Christopher Columbus   Betsie ten Boom   Tony Dungy

8 ATTRIBUTES *of* GREAT ACHIEVERS

VOLUME II

CAMERON C. TAYLOR

Roger Bannister   George Washington   John Wooden

Philo T. Farnsworth   Irena Sendler   Neef Grigg

<u>Other Books by Cameron C. Taylor</u>
Preserve, Protect, & Defend
Does Your Bag Have Holes? 24 Truths That Lead to Financial and Spiritual Freedom
8 Attributes of Great Achievers
Twelve Paradoxes of the Gospel

<u>Author Websites</u>
www.CameronCTaylor.com
www.TheGloriousCauseOfAmerica.org

Table of Contents

INTRODUCTION

This book will help you develop the character attributes that lead to greater achievement. In determining what makes organizations great, Jim Collins, author of *Good to Great*, discovered that the "good-to-great companies placed greater weight on character attributes than on specific educational background, practical skills, specialized knowledge, or work experience."[1] Working to perfect the character attributes discussed in this book will help you achieve sustained, superior performance by developing your most valuable resource—you.

The key to changing how we act and live is to change the attributes we possess. Often, people try to correct behavior when behavior is not the real problem. In the words of Henry David Thoreau, "There are a thousand hacking at the branches of evil to one who is striking at the root."[2] Our behaviors stem from the attributes we possess. Thus, if we want to make lasting change and improvements in our lives, we need to develop the attributes that lead to the behaviors and life we desire.

Each of the attributes of great achievers can be developed, but obtaining the attributes requires more than knowledge and belief. Gandhi once said, "There are 999 who believe in honesty for every honest man." For the principle of honesty to really impact your life, it must become more than something you know: it must be something you are—it must be an attribute you possess. May we each spend the time in study and practice to develop and live the attributes of great achievers.

Enjoy the book.

ATTRIBUTE 9

COURAGE

"Don't let the sensation of fear convince you that you're too weak to have courage. Fear is the opportunity for courage, not proof of cowardice."

-JOHN MCCAIN

CHAPTER I

THE COURAGEOUS RESCUES OF IRENA SENDLER

On September 1, 1939, Nazi Germany invaded Poland, took control of the country, and began separating the Jews from the rest of the population. To create an area to hold the Jews, the Nazis used Jews as slave labor to build a ten foot wall, topped with barbed wire, around a 1.3 square-mile area in the city of Warsaw. This area became known as the Warsaw Ghetto. The wall was completed in the fall of 1940, and over four hundred thousand Jews were forced inside. The Jews were only allowed to carry a small sack into the ghetto and were forced to leave everything else behind. There was not room to accommodate all of the relocated Jews. It thus became normal for seven or eight people to live in each room of a home, and thousands had no home at all. The sidewalks were crowded and overflowed with people.

Guards were stationed at the twenty-two gates in and out of the ghetto, and any Jew found outside of the walls was shot. With the Jews separated from society, the Nazis issued a decree to begin rationing food. The Germans were given 2,613 calories a day and the Jews only 184 calories a day, forcing the Jews to smuggle food into the ghetto to survive.

Irena Sendler was a twenty-nine-year-old Polish social worker over epidemic control. Irena's position allowed her to visit the ghetto. She entered the ghetto on the premise that she was working to prevent the spread of contagious diseases. Secretly, she smuggled in food, clothing, and forged documents to the Jews. Irena smuggled in clothing by wearing many layers. Once safely inside the ghetto, she removed the extra layers to give to those in need. Forged documents and money were sewn into the lining of her clothing or hidden in the false bottom of her nurse bag, which she filled with soiled bandages to discourage the bag from being searched.

Irena watched as thousands of Jews died of starvation. "One family in particular caught her attention—their sole possessions seemed to be two baby strollers. The father pushed three children in one, while the mother pushed three more in another. They sang old Yiddish songs, and their voices were beautiful. Over that first winter, Irena gave them a few coins every day and listened to their singing. After some months she noticed that the mother and father were accompanied by only four children, and then three; eventually one stroller disappeared, as did the family's shoes and their coats. Finally, only the father and mother were left. They still managed to sing, but the mother was skeletal and weak, and the father had to push her in the stroller. Then she too was gone, and there was no more singing."[3]

Irena realized that the only hope of saving these people was to get them out of the ghetto. She knew the task would be difficult and filled with great risk. Every Pole knew what happened to families who were caught helping the Jews. "According to eyewitnesses, the family would be lined up in the street, in full view of their neighbors. First the father was shot, then the mother was made to watch as her children were killed one at a time—first the Jewish children the family had been hiding, then her own. Finally, the mother was executed. Their bodies were left in the street as a warning to the other Poles until the morgue wagon came for them the next day."[4]

Irena developed a plan to rescue children from the ghetto. She would need forged documents to create new Aryan names and identities for each child smuggled out, and she would need to find families willing to take in a Jewish child. With the sources for documents and leads to foster families in place, Irena searched for methods to smuggle the children past the guards. There was a courthouse that straddled the wall of the ghetto. One side of the courthouse was within the ghetto, and the other side was in Aryan Warsaw. Irena obtained the help of a janitor at the courthouse who unlocked passageways to allow her and the children to enter and exit undetected.

Irena smuggled out three to four orphans a week and placed them with foster families, orphanages, and various convents. Irena wanted to be sure that following the war each child's real name was restored, so they could be reunited with any surviving relatives. Though many believed that keeping the list of names was too risky, Irena insisted that the names be preserved. They knew that if the list were found, it would be a death sentence for each of the Jewish children and the families or organizations assisting them. However, she believed that all the children deserved to know their real name and the names of their families. She took the lists to a friend's home and buried the names in a glass jar under an apple tree. The holes were dug in the middle of the night using a kitchen knife and a spoon so as to be as quiet as possible. She returned numerous times throughout the war to bury additional names of those rescued.

When one of Irena's couriers, a nineteen-year-old girl named Helena, was captured by the Nazis while smuggling a four-year-old orphan out of the courthouse, the rescue efforts were temporarily suspended. Helena was taken to prison and tortured. Irena felt totally responsible for Helena's imprisonment, believing she should have insisted on more precautions. She was also concerned that the Nazis had knowledge of her network and rescue efforts.

Each day, the Nazis placed posters with the names of individuals executed for assisting the Jews. Two days after Helena's arrest, her name appeared on the poster. Irena waited for a week following Helena's arrest to see if the Gestapo would come for her or others in their network. The Gestapo never came and the rescue efforts resumed. With the locks at the courthouse changed, they had to develop new methods to smuggle out the children.

Some of the children were sedated and placed among the corpses taken by the morgue wagon from the ghetto. Infants were smuggled in the bottom of a toolbox. Using an ambulance, they were able to hide children under the stretcher. Paths outside the ghetto through underground sewer pipes and other secret underground passages were developed. One boy who was near death from starvation was so skinny he was able to climb inside the pants of a man and hold on to his belt as the man walked out of the ghetto undetected. Eventually, the courthouse was used again to smuggle out children.

Their rescue efforts were saving five to ten children each week, when the Nazi decree came ordering the deportation of all Jews in the Warsaw Ghetto to work camps. The Jews were loaded into trains by the thousands. Word soon came back that those taken from the ghetto were not taken to work camps but were taken to the Nazi extermination camp, Treblinka. The Nazis began deporting Jews from the ghetto at a rate of over five thousand a day.

Irena knew they must do more, and quickly, to save as many children as possible from execution. It required greater risk and an expansion of the network, but through their efforts, they began saving around fifteen children a day. Eventually the ghetto was completely destroyed, and no one was left to save. The Treblinka extermination camp was in operation between July 1942 and October 1943 and resulted in the murder of more than eight hundred thousand Jews.

Irena and her supporting network had rescued two thousand and five hundred children. Irena had secured the name of each child, their new name, and their location in the jars buried under the apple tree. With no more children to save, Irena turned her efforts to supporting the rescued children and the foster families, convents, and orphanages that cared for them.

On October 20, 1943, ten Nazi police and a Gestapo agent poured into Irena's apartment and began to ransack each room. One soldier held Irena and the others in the apartment at gunpoint while the Nazis emptied drawers, cut open mattresses and pillows, and searched closets and cabinets. After their search was complete, the police took Irena from the apartment and forced her into the back of a police wagon. Irena was taken to Pawiak Prison, given a gray-and-black-striped uniform, and placed in a cell with seven other women. The cell was only eight feet by twelve feet with two small beds and no window. Irena was assigned to work in the laundry where she stood at a sink for twelve hours a day scrubbing underwear with a wire brush.

Each morning the prisoners were lined up, and names were called for execution. Irena had been sentenced to death, but her name was not called. Instead, she was taken to an interrogation room and strapped to a chair. Irena had been told that several confessions regarding the removal of Jewish children from the ghetto had been obtained and that in each account her name was mentioned. Irena's interrogator demanded to know their leaders, code names, escape routes, and the names and addresses of others involved.

Irena tried to convince her interrogator that she didn't know anything, but he replied that it was her life or his. He was going to make her tell him what she knew. The beating began with the interrogator hitting her legs and feet with a club. Then he pulled out a whip and began to lash her legs and feet with such force that each strike slashed through her skin. After an hour of torture, the interrogator signaled for her release. The torture was repeated each day for an hour, with the interrogator asking the same questions again and again. Irena knew she had to be strong. She wrote, "If I broke down [all the children were] at risk."[5] Every morning Irena scratched a line on the wall of her cell, decided which pleasant childhood memory she would focus on during the torture, and committed to be strong for one more day.

The torture resulted in multiple fractures in her legs and feet. The interrogator would use the injuries of the previous beatings as a target to intensify the pain. "On Irena's 35th day she endured a particularly vicious beating. . . . Irena lost consciousness and regained awareness on the cement floor of the toilet room, lying in her own dried blood."[6]

The cruelty of the prison guards was abhorrent. Irena watched as women were pulled from the laundry room and shot. She witnessed guards randomly shoot their pistols into the peepholes of crowded cells. She watched in horror and disbelief as one guard gave a three- or four-year-old Jewish boy a piece of candy, patted the boy on the head, pulled out his pistol and shot the child in the back as he walked away.

At the end of December, after more than two months in prison, one of her cellmates was among those called for execution. She was "a sweet soft-spoken grandmotherly woman, about the same age as Irena's mother."[7] She gave one final gift to Irena before her execution—a small picture of Jesus with the words written on the back, "In Jesus We Trust." Irena hid it next to her heart. When she looked at the picture of Jesus, she thought of her cellmate and the power of love she represented, even in this horrible place, and it gave her a small measure of peace and courage.[8]

On the morning of January 20, 1944, Irena lined up with the other prisoners for the hundredth time. She heard her name called for execution. "In the moment before the guard dragged her out of line, Irena pressed the picture of Jesus into the hand of the newest inmate in her cell, a young mother arrested for smuggling. The woman had been crying for two days, [worried] that she would never see her children again. As Irena was led away with the others selected to die that day, Irena told her, 'For the sake of your children, be brave and strong.'"[9]

Irena was taken with approximately fifteen other women. She was in constant pain and could barely walk. The fifteen women were taken inside the lobby of a building where each name was called again. As their names were called, they were taken through a door to the left. Shortly after they passed through the door, a gunshot was heard. One of the remaining women fainted; others began crying and praying. When Irena's name was called, she was taken by a German SS officer through a door to the right. Irena thought she was being taken for another beating and asked to be taken to the other door to be shot. Irena wrote, "Death would be a relief—less to fear than one more beating. I had not divulged any names or any details about our network or the children's lists."[10]

The officer pushed Irena into a room, and she fell to the ground. Her legs, throbbing from the many beatings, were so swollen that she thought her skin would burst. The officer grasped Irena forcefully by the arm, lifted her from the floor, and took her to another door. The officer unlocked the door, led her into an alleyway, and hurried her across various streets. Her legs burned with pain. Irena was confused as she felt the chill of the crisp January morning. The sun blinded her as she had not seen it for a hundred days.

As they rounded a corner onto a quiet street, the officer released his brutal grip and said, "You are free. Get out of here as fast as you can." Irena leaned against a street lamp thinking she was dreaming or already dead. The officer shook her by the shoulders saying, "Don't you understand? Get out of here." In response, Irena asked for her papers. The officer hit her across the face and walked away. As Irena fell to the ground, she could taste the blood from the strike. She struggled to pull herself to her feet and limped to a pharmacy a few doors away. A young woman looked up from the counter with an expression of shock and horror. She helped Irena to the back of the store where she gave her a glass of water and some medicine. She provided Irena with some old clothing, combed her knotted and matted hair as best she could, and doused her in cologne to mask the stench of Irena's body odor. The young woman gave Irena a cane and money for the tram. Irena rested at the pharmacy for an hour to gain strength to catch the tram home.[11]

The next day Irena walked with the aid of two canes. She hobbled to one of the recently hung red wall posters that announced those who had been executed the day before. Irena saw her name on the list, along with seventeen others, and her crime listed as "aiding and abetting Jews, consorting with underground elements."

She contacted those she had worked with in rescuing children and learned they had paid a large bribe to an officer at the prison for her release. Irena desperately desired to resume her work helping children. While in hiding for the remainder of the war, Irena resumed her work supporting the rescued children. She slept at different houses each night, and for a few days, she stayed at the Warsaw Zoo as the guest of the zookeeper. Her companions in the zoo were an armadillo and a baby fox. At the conclusion of the war, Irena returned to the apple tree to retrieve the buried jars filled with the names of the rescued children.

In interviews later in life, Irena expressed great fear that the memory of the Holocaust would be forgotten. It was very painful for Irena to share her story and to relive painful memories, but she knew it was necessary so that these horrors would not happen again. Irena declared, "My greatest fear is that after the last survivor is gone, memory of the Holocaust will disappear. This pain is greater than the pain in my leg."[12] The philosopher George Santayana wrote, "Those who cannot remember the past are condemned to repeat it."

Irena was often asked if she was afraid. She answered, "Yes. I was afraid but . . . it was a need of my heart. . . . I can't bear the suffering, and no one suffered as much as the Jewish children. It's just the decent thing to do."[13] "During the war we intended to defeat Hitler and the Nazis. And we did. Anything is possible. You just have to do the right thing— one foot after another."[14] "Don't let the sensation of fear convince you that you're too weak to have courage. Fear is the opportunity for courage."[15]

When Irena was asked why she led such a risky rescue effort, she shared a story from her youth. When she was seven years old, her father was in the hospital with typhus, and she went to visit him with her mother. Her father called Irena to his side and said, "Irena. Always remember what I've taught you. People are all the same. . . . Always remember, my darling Irena. If you see someone drowning, you must rescue him."[16] She answered, "I'll remember, father."[17] Her father died five days later.

Irena Sendler was just four feet and eleven inches tall and weighed less than one hundred pounds, but her courage was inversely proportional to her physical stature. She remembered the words of her dying father, and she rescued many who were drowning. Although she passed away on May 12, 2008, at the age of ninety-eight, her example of courage lives on. We must have in our memory models of courage like Irena Sendler to give us the strength to act even when we are afraid.

ATTRIBUTE 10
LOVE

"I know how difficult it is to follow this grand law of love. But are not all great and good things difficult to do? . . . Whether mankind will consciously follow the law of love, I do not know. But that need not disturb us. The law will work just as the law of gravitation works whether we accept it or not."

-MAHATMA GANDHI

CHAPTER II

THE 6 LOVE LANGUAGES OF BUSINESS AND LIFE

"Love is the ultimate and the highest goal to which man can aspire."

-Victor E. Frankl

Love is the great facilitator of leadership—the *sine qua non*. *Sine qua non* is a Latin phrase meaning "without which not." If love is not present, true leadership will not occur. "When we truly love others without condition, without strings, we help them feel secure and safe and validated and affirmed in their essential worth, identity, and integrity. Their natural growth process is encouraged. We make it easier for them to live the laws of life—cooperation, contribution, self-discipline, integrity—and to discover and live true to the highest and best within them."[18] There is nothing more powerful than the principle of unconditional love when influencing others for good.

Just as it requires work and effort to cultivate a garden, it also takes work and effort to cultivate loving relationships. An unattended garden or relationship only grows weeds. The former CEO of General Electric, Jack Welch, knew that he "needed to treat people in a first-class way if he wanted to attract and keep the best."[19] Here are six things you can do to cultivate loving relationships in your professional and personal life.

1. GIVE SINCERE COMPLIMENTS

"I resolve to speak ill of no man . . . and speak all the good I know of everybody."

-Benjamin Franklin

There is great good inside of everyone; you just have to look for it. There is a natural tendency to point out when someone does something wrong and say nothing when they do something good. We must train ourselves to look for the good in people and their actions. Then we must express what we see with a verbal or written compliment and hold our tongue when we are inclined to criticize. People need and want to be complimented. Compliments bring out the best efforts in people by uplifting and motivating them. Even if people make mistakes, focus on their successful efforts and compliment them on those items. "I can't think of any downside to giving compliments. . . . It helps relationships, makes others feel good, and contributes to your own sense of joy. Giving compliments is a great way to make your life, and the lives of others, just a little bit better."[20] Encouragement and compliments are a much more effective teaching device than criticism, so always look for opportunities to compliment those around you.

Charles M. Schwab

> "The best way to develop the best that is in a
> person is by appreciation and encouragement.
> There is nothing else that so kills the ambitions of a
> person as criticisms."
>
> -Charles M. Schwab

"When Charles Schwab took his first job in the steel industry in 1879, he began as a day laborer. He had shown no previous interest in metallurgy, management, or finance, though he had taken a high school course in surveying and engineering. But within six months, at the age of eighteen, he was the acting chief engineer of the largest steel mill in America."[21] In 1897, at the age of thirty-five, Schwab became the president of Carnegie Steel Company. "Four years later, in 1901, he served as the intermediary between Carnegie and J.P. Morgan, helping to bring about the merger which created the first billion-dollar company in America, the United States Steel Corporation. He was U.S. Steel's first president."[22] As a six-percent owner of Carnegie Steel Company at the time of the merger, Schwab received $25 million (approximately $600 million in today's dollars) in bonds in the new corporation.[23]

One of the keys to Schwab's success in business was his ability to give compliments and not criticize. "No one who knew Schwab could recall even a single instance in which he raised his voice in anger, even when his own health or safety had been jeopardized by someone's forgetfulness or carelessness. He believed that people respond best to praise, not criticism, and that when one can find nothing to praise, it is better to keep silent than to condemn."[24]

When Schwab was asked for his secret in leading others he said, "I have yet to find a man, whatever his situation in life, who did not do better work and put forth greater effort under a spirit of approval than he ever would do under a spirit of criticism. I treat men as I want to be treated myself. I never quarrel. If any difference arises I go to a man frankly and reason it out with him. If we disagree, we disagree amicably. Then I encourage men constantly. Every man, no matter how high his position, is susceptible to encouragement. That's the only secret."[25]

James Gasque

Kathleen Parker, a writer for the *Washington Post*, won the Pulitzer Prize. Following this achievement she wrote, "On such occasions, one is expected to recognize those who have helped along the way. . . . [The] scene took place in my 11th-grade English class. . . . The teacher was mine for only three months, but he changed my life in a flicker of light. I materialized in James Gasque's class in March of the school year. . . . I knew no one and had come from a small high school in central Florida where, for some reason, no one had bothered to teach the diagramming of sentences. Thus, my fellow students at Dreher High School in Columbia, S.C., were way ahead of me when Mr. Gasque finally called on me to identify some part of a sentence he had written on the blackboard.

"His back to the class with chalk in hand, he stood poised to write my instructions. Every living soul knows the feeling of helplessness when a crowd of peers awaits the answer you do not know. Whatever I said was utterly ridiculous, I suppose, because my classmates erupted in peals of laughter. I have not forgotten that moment, or the next, during all these years. As I was trying to figure out how to hurl myself under my desk, Mr. Gasque . . . whirled. Suddenly facing the class, he flushed crimson and his voice trembled with rage. 'Don't. You. Ever. Laugh. At her. Again.' he said. 'She can out-write every one of you any day of the week.' It is not possible to describe my gratitude. Time suspended and I dangled languorously from a fluff of cloud while my colleagues drowned in stunned silence. . . . Probably no one but me remembers Mr. Gasque's act of paternal chivalry, but I basked in those words and in the thought that what he said might be true, I started that day to try to write as well as he said I could. I am still trying."[26]

Accepting Compliments

An important exchange occurs when compliments are given and received. When you reject a compliment, you also reject the giver of the compliment. This can create awkward exchanges. Imagine, for example, what would occur if someone handed you a beautifully wrapped present and you handed it back and said, "I don't want it."

For example, during the summer I enjoy boating and waterskiing. A few friends and I were headed out to the lake one day, and as we were in front of my house getting the boat ready, one of them said, "I love your yard. It is beautiful." I replied, "Not really. There are so many weeds and so much trimming that needs to be done." He then said again, "No, really, I like your yard." At this point, I realized I had rejected his compliment, and he was trying to give the compliment again to see if I would accept it on the second attempt. I accepted the compliment with a simple "thank you." As I analyzed why I rejected the first compliment, I realized that it was because I didn't think the yard was worthy or deserving of the compliment. In an attempt to reject the compliment, I came up with reasons that the yard was unworthy and undeserving of the compliment. When we receive personal compliments, we may also try to find reasons we are not worthy or deserving of the compliment and thus reject the compliment. We should graciously accept the compliments that are given to us with a simple "thank you" and accept them for the gifts that they are and seek to give the gift of compliments to others.

2. LISTEN AND BE UNDERSTANDING

What would happen right now if all the air were taken out of the room you are currently in? What would happen to your interest in this book? Air is a fundamental physical need, and until that need is met, you will not be interested in anything else. However, once you have fulfilled the need for air, your interests can shift to other things. What is the emotional and psychological equivalent of air? It is the need to be understood. Why? Because when you understand another person, you fulfill many basic human needs. When you understand a person, you have accepted them. When you listen to understand a person, you are saying, "You are important and I care about you. You are a person worth listening to, a person of significance, a person that matters."

A study was done to see what people desired in a potential partner. Understanding was the number-one characteristic desired by women and the number-two characteristic desired by men. If you desire to communicate effectively with another, you must first understand them. How do we understand another? By listening. Many of your problems with people will disappear and your relationships will be greatly strengthened if you will learn the simple skill of listening first. As Gandhi once said, "Three-fourths of the miseries and misunderstanding in the world will disappear if we step into the shoes of our adversaries and understand their standpoint."

Our feelings and thoughts are based upon how we perceive situations, so we need to make sure we correctly understand the situation before we act. Oftentimes, when we come to understand the situation, how we feel and what we think are greatly changed. As our understanding of the situation changes, so does the message we desire to communicate.

Andy Wilson

Andy Wilson was promoted to become the youngest regional vice president at Walmart. Shortly after moving into the corporate headquarters, Walmart's founder and chairman, Sam Walton, stopped by his office unexpectedly. "Andy quickly rose and shook Sam's hand. Then Sam edged past Andy toward the chair behind his desk [and] said, 'Andy, I want to tell you something and I don't want you to forget it.' Sam patted the back of the now-empty chair. 'Never make a crucial decision sitting in this chair.' Andy nodded respectfully and scribbled down the phrase. . . . Sitting at his desk just a few weeks later, Andy received a call from Rob, a veteran district manager, to let Andy know he would be demoting or firing a store manager. The store was underperforming and a change was needed. Andy was about to agree when he glanced down at his yellow pad of paper and saw the challenge from Sam written there: Never make a crucial decision sitting is this chair. 'Hold on, I'll fly out on Monday,' Andy said. 'Don't do anything yet. I do not know this manager personally.'

"On Monday morning, Rob picked Andy up from the airport. On their drive to the store, Andy countered Rob's readiness to replace the manager by saying that he liked to talk with the associates before firing anyone. So when they arrived, Andy walked around the store, asking associates about the manager. It didn't take long to find out that he was indeed struggling in his job—but also struggling to care for his wife, who was ill with cancer, and their two children. He was overwhelmed. Andy went to the front of the store and called Rob over the intercom . . . Andy asked, 'What's the manager's wife's name?' Rob didn't know. 'Any ideas on why he's struggling?' Rob didn't have any. . . Andy quickly related what he had learned and said, 'We are not going to fire this man just because he's going through a hard time.' . . . Andy called all of the associates together and brought the store manager to the front. He addressed the workers: 'We need you to rally around him. We're going to give him as much time as he needs to be with his wife and family. In the meantime, there will be an interim manager, but we ask that you pitch in and give a little more to help this store thrive.' Ultimately, the store manager's wife returned to good health, and he was able to return to his store manager position, where he is very effective today."27

Tony Dungy

Tony Dungy, then coach for the Tampa Bay Buccaneers, shares this story about a series of games where their placekicker, Michael Husted, missed several field goals. Dungy wrote, "Michael's mother was battling cancer . . . cancer that ultimately took her life. Michael was a very private person, and while the team knew about his mom, the press and the public were unaware of what he was dealing with. He was getting criticized for missing kicks, and I was getting criticized for not replacing him. . . . Even though he was missing kicks he would ordinarily make, I decided I was not going to replace him. While this was hurting the team in the short run . . . I was certain that we'd be better as a unit for standing beside one of our own members through a difficult time. I told the team during a meeting, 'Michael is going through some tough times on and off the field. But I don't care how many kicks he misses along the way; he will remain our kicker. If he misses, we'll need to rise up and get the ball back. But before it's all said and done, he's going to make some big kicks for us.' In the years since then, Michael has expressed his appreciation for my sticking with him during that time. I didn't do anything special. I just treated him the way I would want to be treated. Even at the time, this made quite an impact on him and on the other players. Michael went on to kick well for the rest of the season."[28]

Cameron C. Taylor

I had an employee in one of my companies who was making mistakes and not completing work. She had been a fantastic employee, so I thought it was just an aberration and that it would not continue. However the mistakes and uncompleted work continued. I began receiving concerns regarding her work from others in the company, and I knew it couldn't wait any longer. I needed to speak with her. I had a list of all the mistakes and tasks that had not been completed and the negative effect it had on our business. My first reaction was to call her in, go over the list with her, and then tell her these problems needed to be corrected or I would have to hire someone else to do the job.

As the time for our meeting arrived, she came into my office and had a seat. I had the list in front of me, but I then remembered the principle "listen and be understanding" and set aside the list of problems that needed to be corrected and asked, "Tell me how you are doing?" She began to tell me of a close friend that was suddenly killed in a car accident and about the death of a family member just a couple of days later. She then began to cry saying, "I haven't been handling it very well, and I know my work has suffered." I then asked, "Would you like me to give you a blessing?" (I serve as an elder in my church.) She nodded in the affirmative, and I laid my hands upon her head and gave her a blessing from God. After the blessing, she gave me a hug, and I asked if there was anything else I could do to help. She answered, "I would like to take a couple of days off to spend with family and deal with the emotions I am experiencing." I answered, "That will be fine. We will take care of your tasks while you are away."

Upon her return, she did her job well, and I never had to bring up the list of items I had sitting on my desk during our meeting. I am glad I chose to first listen and then respond, for it drastically changed my message to her.

"He that answereth a matter before he heareth it, it is a folly and shame unto him."[29]

3. VIEW PEOPLE BY THEIR POTENTIAL NOT BY THEIR PAST

Don't treat people in terms of their past behavior, but rather in terms of their potential—in terms of what they can become. Goethe put it this way: "Treat a man as he is and he will remain as he is; treat a man as he can and should be, and he will become as he can and should be."

Hal Wing

The founder and CEO of the Little Giant Ladder Company, Hal Wing, shared the following story. It is a powerful example of focusing on a person's future instead of a person's past.

We had a single job opening at our company, and at this time, I was the person making the hiring decision. The production manager brought me a three-inch stack of job applications to review. As he put them on my desk, he said, "You can take the top application and throw it away."

I replied, "Why do you recommend I do that?"

The production manager answered, "The guy is a loser."

I thought that to be a peculiar reason so I inquired, "Did he put loser down on his resume?

"No," was the reply, so I continued, "Well, then how do you know he is loser?"

The production manager explained to me that this applicant was a police officer who was caught stealing things out of people's cars at night, and he spent five years in prison. This sparked my curiosity, so

I examined his application and resume. As I looked at the application, I did not see a criminal. I saw an individual with a good education, a history of service to his community, an eagle scout, a husband, and father of four children. I decided I wanted to meet this man, so I called him up and asked him to come in for an interview.

When he showed up for the interview, I was surprised by what I saw. He was a large man who filled the doorway as he came through. He was big, but he was all muscle. As I talked with him, there was humility in his eyes and a desire to work that I had rarely seen, so I hired him. He did excellent work and needed no supervision. Over the months and years ahead, he received many promotions and raises. One day I went into the factory and found him hard at work as usual.

I walked up to him with a key in my hand and said, "You are going to need this."

He asked, "What is it for?"

I answered, "It is a master key and it opens every door in the building including my office."

He looked at the key and then looked at me and said, "We need to talk." He pulled me back behind a stack of ladders and was looking down at his feet and shuffling around.

I then said, "Wait a minute. Are you trying to tell me that you were once a police officer who was caught stealing, and that you spent five years in prison?"

He looked at me, and tears flowed down his cheeks as he said, "You knew and you still hired me. Why?"

I answered, "Well, I can't even imagine what it would be like to spend five years in prison as a former police officer. I can't image what it would be like to have to tell my children that I am not going to be around for a while because I am going to prison. I can't image what it would be like to try and provide for a wife and four children when no one would hire me because of my past. When you sat across from me in our interview, I saw a man who was truly sorry for what he had done, a man who was remorseful, who was looking for another opportunity to prove himself. I saw in you a humility and a desire to work, which is hard to find."

This big man grabbed me and hugged me tightly. With tears in his eyes he said, "Thank you. Thank you."

This good man worked for me for thirty years until he retired, and he was a tremendous asset to our company, overseeing millions of dollars of inventory.

Cameron C. Taylor

I had applied to be an executive director of a leadership organization at a university. There were many excellent candidates for the position, and I was notified that I was selected as one of three final candidates they would be interviewing. After the final interviews, I received notification that I had been hired for the job. In my first meeting with the man who hired me, he said to my surprise, "You were not the best candidate today for this job. The other two candidates would have both been better at the job on day one, but we see in you the potential to learn and grow and do things in the future that will surpass what the other candidates could have done. We are not hiring you because you are the best executive director today, but because you will be a great executive director in the future."

Opportunity

Upon graduating from business school, I decide to start a business. I was determined to build a multimillion-dollar company, but my business venture failed, leaving me with thousands of dollars in business debt. I was newly married, and I had no income. My wife was working earning $10 per hour, but her income was not even enough to cover our monthly $1,800 debt payments. I now joke with her that she married me for my money, but the truth is, I had less than nothing because of the burden of debt. I was forced to put my entrepreneurial efforts on hold for a season and look for a job. I graduated with honors from business school and applied for dozens of jobs that were a good match for my skills, experience, and degree, but I received rejection letter after rejection letter. I even applied at a call center for a $6-per-hour job that seemed to hire nearly everyone and was rejected. I now joke with people that I had to start a business because I was the only person who would hire me.

I still wanted to start another business, but this did not seem like a possible option at this point in my life. At this time, I was volunteering at the local university, running a lecture series that I taught with invited guests. Following one of the lectures by an invited guest, a miracle happened. It was about one and a half hours after the lecture had ended. I had stayed to talk with students and answer questions. When I exited the building, the guest lecturer pulled up next to me in the parking lot. He rolled down his window and said, "We need to talk." We set up a time to meet the next week. We began not sure exactly why we were meeting. He laid out the projects he was working on and ideas he wanted to pursue. I laid out my talents, experience, and the projects I was working on and wanted to pursue. We eventually came to a business idea that felt like the right one. We partnered on the new venture, with him putting up all the money and me putting up the time to build and manage the company. He said to me, "I see in you great potential, and I believe that with the right opportunity and resources you will do amazing things." The company did over $1 million in revenue the second year in business and over $10 million in the fifth year of business.

I am grateful that he gave me a shot at a time in my life when I could not even get hired at the $6-per-hour customer service call center. I am so glad that he did not judge me on my past or my current situation, but on what I could become.

4. GIVE GIFTS

"Gift giving is a fundamental expression of love that transcends cultural barriers. . . . A gift is something you can hold in your hand and say, 'Look, he was thinking of me,' or 'She remembered me.' You must be thinking of someone to give him a gift. The gift itself is a symbol of that thought. . . . From early years, children are inclined to give gifts to their parents, which may be another indication that gift giving is fundamental to love. Gifts are visual symbols of love."[30]

To become a good gift giver requires effort. Think for a moment on these questions. What are the best gifts you have received? What are the best gifts you have given? How can you have this positive gift-giving experience more often? One key is to be observant as to what people like and the things they may want. Throughout your interaction with others, you will pick up whether they like the ballet or sporting events, what foods they like, what their favorite restaurants are, where they like to shop, etc. "Showing appreciation through tangible gifts is effective when the gift shows that the giver has spent time and energy thinking about the gift. They have answered the questions, 'What would this person enjoy? What are their interests? What would make them feel special and appreciated?'"[31]

"Thoughtless gifts—those gifts bought hastily in response to tradition or a feeling of obligation—with no real personal investment of time or reflection not only miss the mark but also communicate a negative message."[32]

I have tried to apply the principle of gift giving in each of my companies. Every client receives a gift and thank-you note for purchasing. Every organization we partner with receives a handwritten thank-you note and gift in the mail. Our employees receive gifts on their birthdays and other occasions. Every customer who has a complaint or problem with our company receives a gift.

One of our clients, Dr. Wilk, sent an e-mail accusing our company of not refunding his money for merchandise he had returned. He demanded his money with interest and threatened to report us to the Better Business Bureau as a scam. He had also sent this e-mail to the director of his professional association with whom we had a relationship. I worked directly with the director of this association, so I personally looked into the matter and found that his money had been returned shortly after we received the merchandise. I replied to his e-mail, and I copied the reply to the director of his professional association, explaining when the money was returned and how he could verify it.

I then wrote: "I apologize for the miscommunication. I have put a gift to you in the mail to apologize for the mistake. Let me know if you have any other concerns, and I will make sure they get taken care of." Dr. Wilk sent me an e-mail thanking me for the gift, and I received an e-mail from the director of the association, which read:

> "Dear Cameron,
> Thank you for your continued patience and kindness. I did learn just recently that Dr. Wilk lost a son in just the past few months to a long and horrible death from a brain tumor. His son was only in his early 40s and folks here have said Dr. Wilk has slowed a little. So again, thanks for taking the extra time.
>
> Take care, M----"

The Accidental Gift

My wife, Paula, is one of the most loving, friendly, outgoing people I know. A few years ago she was several months pregnant and was in a car accident. She was stopped at a traffic light when a person three cars back failed to stop causing a four-car accident. My wife did not have her insurance information with her, so she called me and asked me to bring it to her. When I arrived with the insurance information, the police were taking statements and information. The drivers of the other damaged cars were upset and angry, but Paula was happy and was making friends. Paula went up to the driver responsible for the accident and gave her a hug and said, "You need a present." My wife then handed her a present she had in the car. The girl said in shock, "I damaged your car and caused you and your baby a great deal of stress, and you're giving me a present?"

5. FORGIVE

One of my mentors shared the following story about a group of teenagers who went for a picnic in the desert outside of Phoenix. While they were playing, a rattlesnake bit one of the girls on the ankle. The girl and her friends pursued the snake and after about twenty minutes were able to find the snake and kill it. Once the snake was destroyed, they headed to the emergency room. A couple of days later her foot and leg had swollen almost beyond recognition. The tissues in her limb had been destroyed by the poison, and a few days later her leg would be amputated below the knee. It was a senseless sacrifice, the price of revenge. How much better it would have been if after the young woman had been bitten, there had been an extraction of the venom.[33] It is difficult for us to forgive those who have injured us. Dwelling on the wrong done to us becomes an erosive and destructive poison. Nelson Mandela wrote, "Resentment is like drinking poison and then hoping it will kill your enemies."

Business Jon Huntsman wrote, "The only person bitterness bites is the one who holds the grudge. Grudges are physically, emotionally, and mentally draining, [and] unhealthy.... Obsessing on grudges keeps them alive; forgiveness forces them to die. Moving on gets you back to business."[34]

The $10-Million-Dollar Mistake

A man who worked for IBM made a mistake that cost his company $10 million. After making this mistake, the man was called in to meet with the company founder and CEO, Tom Watson Sr. The nervous employee entered the office and took a seat. He sat in silence, waiting for the CEO to speak, but the silence continued. Finally the employee said, "I guess you want my resignation?" The CEO replied, "You can't be serious. We've just spent $10 million educating you!"[35]

Mistakes are a part of life and learning, and thus we should forgive those who have done wrong. We must come to view mistakes not as failure but as learning. We often learn more from our failures than we do from our successes. Success is not a single event but a process. What matters more than where you are is the direction you are heading. "Bill Gates, the founder of Microsoft, has said, 'I like to hire people who have made mistakes. It shows that they take risks.'"[36]

6. PROVIDE RECOGNITION

An extensive and in-depth study on workplace productivity found that "of the people who report the highest morale at work, 94.4 percent agree that their managers are effective at recognition. In contrast, 56 percent of employees who report low morale give their manager a failing grade on recognition and only 2.4 percent of people who have low morale say they have a boss who is great at recognition."[37] This study also found that the companies in the highest quartile of recognition scores report an operating margin six times higher than the companies in the lowest quartile. Being able to effectively provide recognition to those with whom you work will have a great impact on the success of your organization.

"When you think of recognition, what comes to mind? Do you think of raises, bonuses, stock awards, gift certificates, parties, prizes, and plaques? . . . According to employees, 57 percent of the most meaningful recognition is free. Employees are looking for meaning, not things. They see tangible awards as a vehicle for delivering recognition, but they don't regard the awards themselves as recognition. They're much more interested in the underlying message behind the reward. . . . For awards to count as recognition, your employees need to see acknowledgement of their specific accomplishments and sincere appreciation of their personal value to the organization."[38]

Conclusion

To build strong and lasting relationships in business and in life, give sincere compliments, listen and be understanding, view people by their potential and not by their past, give gifts, forgive, and provide recognition.

ATTRIBUTE 11
MASTER OF
FUNDAMENTALS

"Build your empire on the firm
foundation of the fundamentals."

-Lou Holtz

CHAPTER III

THE POWER OF FUNDAMENTALS

"There is no trick, no easy way to achieve
greatness and success in basketball or life. . . .
What I taught was as simple as one, two, three."

-Coach John Wooden

An example of the power of fundamentals comes from one of my students. For the past fifteen years I have been the keynote speaker on goal setting at a leadership training retreat for high school sophomores. A few of the sophomores are selected to return to the next year's retreat to assist as staff. One of the students who returned shared his experience with goal setting over the last year. He told me of all the wonderful things he accomplished. His parents, teachers, and classmates began to ask what had changed and what made it possible for him to accomplish so much over the past year.

He responded to their questions by saying he began writing down his goals and working to achieve them. He said that most of those who inquired were very surprised by his simple answer. Goal setting is a simple, fundamental process that produces a dramatic increase in what you can accomplish, yet 97 percent of people do not do it. Studies have found that only 3 percent of Americans have written goals.

Coach Chuck Noll taught, "Champions are champions not because they do anything extraordinary but because they do the ordinary things better than anyone else."[39] It is the small and simple tasks that produce the great results. "The great truths in life are the simple ones."[40] "Success in life is founded upon attention to the small things rather than to the large things; to the everyday things nearest to us rather than to the things that are remote and uncommon."[41]

Coach John Wooden—Teacher of Fundamentals

John Wooden was born in the small town of Hall, Indiana, in 1910. Just before his twenty-second birthday he began his basketball coaching career at Dayton High School in Kentucky. They finished with six wins and eleven losses for the year. This was Coach Wooden's only season in which his team had a losing record. After two years at Dayton, he returned to Indiana where he took a job at South Bend Central High School as an English teacher and coach of the basketball, baseball, and tennis teams. During his eleven years coaching high school basketball, Coach Wooden had an impressive 218-42 record.

Coach left South Bend Central after nine years to serve as a lieutenant in the US Navy during World War II. In 1946 following the war, Coach Wooden took a job at Indiana State University as the athletic director as well as the basketball and baseball coach. Under Coach Wooden, Indiana State won conference championships in 1946 and 1947 and finished as runner-up in the 1947 NAIA tournament.

Shortly after the NAIA tournament, Coach Wooden received a number of coaching offers at larger schools. One of the offers came from UCLA. Coach wrote, "Immediately after accepting the position, I arranged to take a week off from Indiana State to go to Los Angeles to conduct spring basketball practice, which was then permitted. On my previous visit I had been all over the campus, visited various administrators and officials, but had not met one of the basketball players. When I went up on the floor for the first time in the spring of 1948 and put them through that first practice, I was very disappointed. I felt my Indiana State team could have named the score against them. I was shattered. Had I known how to abort the agreement in an honorable manner, I would have done so. . . . However, that would be contrary to my creed. I don't believe in quitting, so I resolved to work hard [and] try to develop the talent on hand. . . .

"After the close of school at Indiana State, I moved my family to Los Angeles, realizing that I had a tremendous job ahead to turn things around. By the time regular practice started, the press had already tabbed us to finish last in the old Pacific Coast Conference. The year before UCLA won 12 and lost 13, and as far as I could determine the three best players . . . were gone. It was like starting from scratch. Almost all of the early practice sessions were devoted to fundamentals, drills, conditioning, and trying to put my philosophy over. Within a few weeks things didn't look quite as dark. . . . We turned things around . . . and won the Southern Division title with a 10 and 2 record. In all, we won 22 and lost 7 for the full season—the most wins any UCLA team had ever compiled in history."[42]

This was the beginning of many accomplishments at UCLA for Coach Wooden; however, it took time to develop a national championship team. Even though UCLA won the division or conference title six times, they lost in the first round of the NCAA tournament in their first three appearances in 1950, 1952, and 1956.

Coach Wooden wrote, "It takes time to create excellence. If it could be done quickly, more people would do it."[43] After Coach Wooden's arrival at UCLA, it was sixteen years before they won their first national championship in 1964. In 1965, UCLA defeated Michigan in the NCAA championship to win its second straight title.

Coach Wooden wrote of his first two championships, "Suddenly, or so it seemed to some, I was an overnight success with two national basketball titles. The truth is that it took about fifty years."[44] Over the final twelve years of Wooden's coaching career, UCLA won ten national championships.

So what was Coach Wooden's secret to success? Coach Wooden taught, "When I'm asked how players under my supervision won ten national championships in twelve years, here's the best answer I can give. I don't rate myself too high as a 'game' coach, but I was among the best when it came to conducting practice. And practice is where a championship is won.... Little things done well is probably the greatest secret to success.... If you do enough small things right, big things can happen."[45]

Coach Wooden focused on teaching and practicing the fundamentals. He wrote, "I believe in the basics: attention to, and perfection of, tiny details that might commonly be overlooked. They may seem trivial, perhaps even laughable to those who don't understand, but they aren't. They are fundamental to your progress in basketball, business and life. They are the difference between champions and near-champions. . . . There are little details in everything you do, and if you get away from any one of the little details, you're not teaching the thing as a whole. For it is the little things, which, taken together, make the whole. . . . Little things make the big things happen. In fact . . . there are no big things, only a logical accumulation of little things done at a very high standard of performance."[46]

Wooden said that there were many who laughed at his repeated focus on, and perfection of, the small, simple, and basic fundamentals. He wrote, "But I wasn't laughing. I knew very well [they] were the foundation for UCLA's success."[47]

Bill Walton wrote, "Coach Wooden broke it down so the players could master the fundamentals and therefore could play up to their full potential. That's the thing I remember about UCLA basketball. The practices were more important to me than the games. . . . I remember those simple fundamentals . . . and everything else would take care of itself."[48] "[Gail] Goodrich, who played on UCLA's 30-0 national championship team in 1964, said that he knew he wanted to be a Bruin after he saw his first UCLA practice while still in high school. 'I had never seen anything so organized and precise in my life.'"[49]

Carroll Adams said of Coach's practices, "He just drilled you on the strict fundamentals, and when that situation came up in a ball game, you handled it because it had become second nature to you."[50] George Stanich recalls that at UCLA, "The practices were the most important thing. Doing the little things."[51]

"From time to time, other coaches or sportswriters would say that UCLA's basketball teams were much too predictable. . . . Everyone knew what they were going to try to do, but they did it so well that no one could stop them anyway! . . . When he was told that others call his offense 'predictable,' Coach simply said, 'I am not a strategy coach. I'm a practice coach.'. . . Coach drilled the fundamentals into his players."[52] John Green, an All-American at UCLA, said, "Coach used the same plays year after year. Everybody knew what we were going to do, but very few could stop us. That's because Coach had us do things over and over again until we did them right."[53]

"Ex-UCLA basketball coach Jim Harrick said, 'John Wooden . . . emphasized that basketball is a very simple game. . . . You learn to win games from 3:00 to 5:30 every day at practice, certainly not the night of the game.'"[54]

In 1975, during Coach Wooden's final season, Myron Finkbeiner recalls watching the Bruins practice during the Final Four. "It was amazing to watch them, because Coach put them through the same drills he had used on the first day of practice at the beginning of the season. They ran through simple passing drills, pivoting moves, blocking-out routines. John Wooden was redoing the fundamentals all over again."[55] UCLA went on to win its tenth national championship. After forty years of coaching, Wooden continued to focus on, teach, and practice the simple fundamentals, for they were the source of his success. Coach lived his words: "Do the basics right, and do as well as you can with what God gave you, and you will be surprised at how far you can get in life. . . . Little things make big things happen."[56]

Conclusion

We have a natural tendency to try and complicate simple solutions and principles, or to doubt their effectiveness. College coaching great Abe Lemons wrote, "I think people try to read something complicated into John Wooden's life, but I think it's so simple that people can't believe it."[57]

CAMERON C. TAYLOR

CHAPTER IV
THE DANGERS OF VAIN OPTIMISM

The long-term effects of various approaches to life can be powerfully illustrated by prison camps "where everyday human nature, stripped bare, can be studied under a magnifying glass of accelerated time. Lessons spotlighted and absorbed in that laboratory sharpen one's eye for their abstruse but highly relevant applications in the 'real time' world of now."[58]

On September 9, 1965, during a mission in the Vietnam War, Admiral Stockdale was taken as a prisoner of war. During his seven and a half years in the Hoa Lo Prison (Hoa Lo means fiery furnace in Vietnamese), Admiral Stockdale was left in solitary confinement for four years, kept in leg irons for two years, malnourished, and physically tortured more than twenty times, having his shoulders wrenched from their sockets, his leg shattered, and his back broken. Stockdale, one of the most highly decorated officers in the history of the navy, received twenty-six combat decorations, including the Medal of Honor (the nation's highest medal for valor).

In his book, *Good to Great*, Jim Collins shares a discussion he had with Admiral Stockdale. As they were discussing Admiral Stockdale's experience as a prisoner of war, Collins asked, "Who didn't make it out?"

"Oh that's easy," replied Admiral Stockdale, "the optimists."

Jim replied, "The optimists? I don't understand."

Admiral Stockdale answered, "The optimists. Oh, they were the ones who said, 'We're going to be out by Christmas.' And Christmas would come and Christmas would go. Then they'd say, 'We're going to be out by Easter.' And Easter would come, and Easter would go. And then Thanksgiving, and then it would be Christmas again. And they died of a broken heart."[59]

Another example was recorded during World War II in one of the prison camps of Nazi Germany. In February 1945, a composer, who was fairly well known throughout the camp, believed that on March 30th he would be liberated and his sufferings ended. He was "full of hope and convinced his dream would be right. But as the day drew nearer, the war news which reached our camp made it appear very unlikely that we would be free on the promised date. On March 29th, [the composer] became ill and ran a high temperature. On March 30th . . . he became delirious and lost consciousness. On March 31st, he was dead."[60]

I have coined the term "vain optimist" to describe the approach of these prisoners. While vain optimism provided a temporary hope to the prisoners, the end result was the breaking of their will and death.

What was different about Admiral Stockdale's approach and attitude as a prisoner of war that enabled him to survive? While the vain optimists put their faith and hope in the false idea of a rescue by a specific day, Admiral Stockdale identified the facts of the situation and acknowledged that it may be years until his release. Admiral Stockdale had a goal to go home, but it was not set to a specific timeline. His goal was to survive until it was over. Each day was considered a victory for he had survived another day. Admiral Stockdale endured 2,712 days in prison until the goal of going home was achieved on February 12, 1973.

Vain Optimism in Success Literature

Contained within some of the new age, self-help, and success literature are the teachings of vain optimism. These books falsely teach that success is solely a result of a person's thoughts with a disregard for truth. While the ideas of vain optimism are found in many success books, I found that the book and DVD entitled *The Secret* provided very clear examples of vain optimism. I have selected a few direct quotes from *The Secret* to illustrate why these teachings are false and dangerous.

The Secret by Rhonda Byrne is a ninety-minute DVD and a two-hundred-page book, which is a transcription of the DVD with additional content. *The Secret* claims to reveal for the first time all the pieces to achieve success. *The Secret* was released in 2006 and has become a worldwide craze, selling millions of copies. The developers of *The Secret* book and video are much like the dishonest trader in the following story who took advantage of the Blackfeet tribe of American Indians. The story goes as follows:

A trader went to a certain Indian nation to dispose of a stock of goods. Among other things he had a quantity of gunpowder. The Indians traded for his clothes, hats, axes, beads, and other things, but would not take the powder saying: "We do not wish for the powder; we have plenty." The trader did not like to carry all the powder back to this camp, so he thought he would play a trick on the Indians, and induce them to buy it. Going to an open piece of ground near the Indian camp he dug up the soft, rich soil; then mixing a quantity of onion seed with his powder, he began to plant it.

The Indians were curious to know what he was doing and stood by greatly interested. "What are you doing?" said one. "Planting gunpowder," replied the trader. "Why do you plant it?" inquired another. "To raise a crop of powder. How could I raise it without planting?" said the trader. "Do you not plant corn in the ground?"

"And will gunpowder grow like corn?" exclaimed half a dozen at once. "Certainly it will," said the trader. "Did you not know it? As you do not want my powder, I thought I would plant it and raise a crop which I could gather and sell to the Crows."

Now the Crows were another tribe of Indians which was always at war with this tribe (the Blackfeet). The idea of their enemies having a large supply of powder increased the excitement, and one of the Indians said; "Well, well, if we can raise powder like corn, we will buy your stock and plant it." But some of the Indians thought best to wait, and see if the seed would grow. So the trader agreed to wait a few days.

In about a week the tiny sprouts of the onion seed began to appear above the ground. The trader, calling the Indians to the spot, said, "You see now for yourselves. The powder already begins to grow, just as

I told you it would." The fact that some small plants appeared where the trader had put the gunpowder was enough to convince the Indians. Every one of them became anxious to raise a crop of gunpowder. The trader sold them his stock, in which there was a large mixture of onion seeds, at a very high price and then left. From this time the Indians gave no attention to their corn crop. If they could raise gunpowder they would be happy.[61]

Just as the trader lied to the Indians and promised a gunpowder harvest to get the Indians' money, so do the creators of *The Secret* profit from the selling of vain optimism. The trader mixed in onion seed to give the illusion of growth and to mask his lies. Likewise, the teachings of vain optimism in *The Secret* are mixed with truth.

The Secret promotes believing and doing things based on false ideas, just like planting gunpowder. Then, when there is no success, blame is placed on the person for not having enough belief in the false teaching. The end result to this approach in the prison camp was repeated disappointment and eventual death. The results of applying "the secret" in other aspects of life will be much the same: repeated disappointment, self-blame, and eventual death of our ambitions.

Vain Optimist Teaching # 1: "Whatever the mind... can conceive it can achieve."[62]

The Indians conceived the idea that you can grow gunpowder and believed that the planted gunpowder would grow. According to the teaching "whatever the mind . . . can conceive it can achieve" the Indians should have had a great gunpowder harvest. Obviously this was not the case.

Vain Optimist Teaching #2: You can defy the laws of nature with your thoughts.

The Secret claims, "The law responds to your thoughts, no matter what they may be."[63] For example, The Secret teaches, "Food is not responsible for putting on weight. It is your thought that food is responsible for putting on weight that actually has food put on weight. . . . Food cannot cause you to put on weight unless you think it can."[64] This is as absurd as saying, "You will only die of dehydration if you think you will. If you think you can live months without water you can." This false claim of weight loss from thinking greatly appeals to many because it requires no work or exercise and allows you to eat whatever you want and as much as you want.

The Secret's formula for getting out of debt is just as ridiculous as its formula for weight loss. You simply have to change your thinking by saying to yourself, "'I can afford that. I can buy that.' . . . Say it over and over."[65] The truth is that the attitude that you can buy and afford everything you see and want will create more debt as people make purchases on credit. Saying you can afford it doesn't make it so unless you believe "the secret" that purchasing things on credit will only create debt if you think it will.

The Secret also teaches, "Beliefs about aging are all in our minds. . . . You can think your way to the perfect state of health . . . and eternal youth."[66] I guess now that millions have learned this secret, that morticians had better start looking for a different line of work because people are going to stop aging and dying.

The Secret falsely claims that if you don't get what you want instantly, it is your fault, saying, "It takes no time for the Universe to manifest what you want. . . . Any time delay you experience is due to your delay in getting to the place of believing, knowing, and feeling that you already have it."[67] According to *The Secret*, a seed only takes four months to grow to harvest or a tree only takes years to grow tall because you think it does. If you think it will grow instantly, it will.

Vain Optimist Teaching #3: All of life's struggles are a result of your thoughts.

Wouldn't life be better if there were no adversity, pain or opposition? *The Secret* teaches the following: "Up until now you may have been thinking that life is hard and a struggle, and so by the law of attraction you will have experienced life as hard and a struggle. Begin right now to shout to the universe, 'Life is so easy!'"[68]

Given the two scenarios below, which of the two schools would you prefer to attend?

School #1

You are required to study and work. Your grade is based on performance, so some will get A's and others will fail. Only those who fulfill the requirements will earn a degree. It is challenging and at times painful.

School #2

All you have to do is shout to your professor, "school is so easy!" As a result of shouting "school is so easy," you are not required to go to class, do homework, or take tests. Everyone at this school who shouts the phrase, "School is so easy!" receives a degree and graduates with a perfect 4.0 GPA. It is easy. It is free from work, pain, and struggle.

When I have posed these two options at various Universities, many students will choose School #2. I will then ask, "How many would like to have a surgery performed by a graduate of School #2?" Obviously, no hands are raised. If such a medical school existed, everyone would graduate with a perfect score and a medical degree. They could be called doctor, but learning the necessary skills of surgery would not have been achieved; thus, the diploma from such an institution would be worthless. Work, pain, struggle, and failure are part of the necessary education process to produce an individual with the specialized skills of a surgeon.

When work, pain, and struggle are taken out of school, the purpose of school is defeated. Likewise, if work and struggle were taken out of life, it would defeat the purpose of life. Life was not designed to be an existence of endless bliss. Life was designed to create greatness in each of us. *The Secret* falsely claims that you can eliminate all pain, suffering, work, and adversity by changing your thinking.

Vain Optimist Teaching #4: "Like Aladdin's Genie, the law of attraction grants our every command."[69]

The Secret teaches, "It's like having the Universe as your catalog. You flip through it and say, 'I'd like to have this experience and I'd like to have that product and I'd like to have a person like that.' It is you placing your order with the Universe. It's really that easy. . . . You get to choose what you want. . . . You can have, be or do anything, and there are no limits."[70] According to *The Secret*, if you want to be a mermaid and live under water, simply ask the Universe, and like a genie, it will turn you into a mermaid. In the scores of biographies I have read, I have yet to find a person whose success formula was a genie.

Vain Optimist Teaching #5: No work required— the Universe does all the work for you.

The Secret teaches, "How it will happen, how the Universe will bring it to you, is not your concern or job. Allow the Universe to do it for you. When you are trying to work out how it will happen, you are emitting a frequency that contains a lack of faith—that you don't believe. . . . The how is not your part in the Creative Process. . . . If you are in action to try and make it happen, you have slipped backward."[71]

The Secret not only teaches that action and work are not required, but that they are bad because it shows a lack of belief and faith in the Universe to do it for you. *The Secret* book and video claim that Thomas Edison's and the Wright Brother's success came as a result of using "the secret."[72] A simple look at the life of Thomas Edison and the Wright Brothers clearly illustrates they did not practice "the secret." Edison's biographies reveal an incredible work ethic, with him often working sixteen hours a day.[73]

The Wright Brothers' story also reveals an action plan and a great deal of work to make their dreams a reality. In 1899, they began their flight experiments. Over the next four years, the Wright Brothers performed thousands of tests, experiments, and flights. In 1901, they created the world's first wind tunnel and tested over two hundred different wing shapes.[74] Just in the months of September and October 1902 they made over seven hundred and fifty glides.[75] After four years of work, on December 17, 1903, Orville, age thirty-two, and Wilber, age thirty-six, achieved their dream of a controlled, powered flight.

Vain Optimist Teaching #6: "Your job is You. . . . It is imperative that you tend to You first. Attend to your joy first."[76]

The Secret teaches, "What's really important to the whole Secret is feeling good. . . . Sacrifice does not feel good. . . . Sacrifice will eventually lead to resentment. . . . Many people have sacrificed themselves for others, thinking when they sacrifice themselves they are being a good person. Wrong! . . . If it ain't fun, don't do it! . . . If it doesn't feel good, then let it go. . . . The only thing you need to do is feel good now."[77] If selfishness, instant gratification, and a life with no fulfillment are your goal then this is good advice. If you are interested in helping others and building something of long-term value then it is not.

Research has shown that delayed gratification is a skill that contributes to long-term success. To find out the effects of delayed gratification, Professor Michael Mischel "developed a simple experiment. . . . A researcher met with a child and established a reward that the child would like, such as a marshmallow. Children were then offered two of the treats instead of one if they could wait for the researcher to leave and then re-enter the room before eating the treat. The researchers then ran follow-up interviews every five years. . . . It turned out. . . that one's ability to delay gratification is quite a significant predictor of a variety of important long-term outcomes . . . . Learning to delay gratification gives children an edge in coping with life's challenges—an edge that lasts into adulthood."[78] Many fall into the trap of focusing on what they want now instead of what matters most long term. It is important to resist the temptation to lose what matters most long term for the short-term pleasure of something now.

Also, we can't satisfy our human needs by directly seeking to fulfill them. Those who are driven by fear and selfishness will attempt to satisfy their needs first but will find it impossible. The more they make the fulfillment of their own needs the target, the further from this goal they will find themselves. The fulfillment of needs requires the use of the principle of indirection, for the true fulfillment of human needs comes as a result of service to others.

Vain Optimist Teaching #7: Truth is relative.

The Secret teaches, "You have nothing to do but convince yourself of the truth which you desire to see manifested. . . . When you conceive something in your mind, know it is a fact. . . . Whatever you choose is right."[79] According to *The Secret*, truth is whatever you think it is. The irrational nature of this idea is illustrated by the following paraphrased dialog of the ancient Greek philosophers Protagoras and Socrates.

PROTAGORAS: Truth is relative; it is only a matter of opinion.
SOCRATES: You mean that truth is mere subjective opinion?
PROTAGORAS: Exactly. What is true for you is true, and what is true for me, is true for me. Truth is subjective.
SOCRATES: Do you really mean that? That my opinion is true by virtue of it being my opinion?

PROTAGORAS: Indeed I do.

SOCRATES: My opinion is: Truth is absolute, not opinion, and that you, Mr. Protagoras, are absolutely in error. Since this is my opinion, then you must grant that it is true according to your philosophy.

PROTAGORAS: You are quite correct, Socrates.[80]

Returning back to the story at the beginning of the chapter, just because the Indians believed that gunpowder could be planted and grown did not make it so. No matter how genuine one's belief may be in a falsity, it will not change that falsity into truth.

Conclusion

Visualization, mental practice, positive thinking, goal setting, and the laws of attraction are effective tools when used in accordance with the laws of success and nature. Unfortunately much of what is taught in the books and seminars on these topics leads to vain optimism. Just as there are principles that govern nature, such as gravity, there are also principles that govern our happiness, peace, and prosperity. It is by learning and living these principles of success that we experience true success and joy.

After having built a business from an idea to a company with revenue of more than $1 million a month, I was often asked what the secret to my success was. I would reply with the principles I had followed in building my business. I remember on one occasion after I provided my simple response, the inquirer got mad and said something along the lines of, "If you don't want to tell me your secret, just say so," and then walked off. So often we look for a magic secret or new technique that will produce tremendous returns and results. Those seeking the magic secret will never find it—for the secret to success is to continually live and apply basic, simple fundamentals over a long period of time.

ATTRIBUTE 12
HARDWORKING

"I never did anything worth doing by accident, nor did any of my inventions come by accident; they came by work."

-THOMAS EDISON

CHAPTER V
THE REWARDS OF HARD WORK

"Success can be attained in any branch of human labor.
There is always room at the top in every pursuit."

-Andrew Carnegie

Having analyzed the lives of hundreds of great achievers, I have found an underlining attribute of consistent work over a long period of time towards well-defined goals. The following are a few examples of the rewards of hard work.

Neef Grigg—Educated at the School of Hard Work[81]

"When I was young, ambitious, and anxious for success, there didn't seem to be many opportunities, and so I made some of my own."

-Neef Grigg, founder of Ore-Ida

Neef was born and raised on a small cattle and dairy farm in Nampa, Idaho. Neef learned the value of hard work at an early age herding and milking cows. Neef later joked saying, "I milked so many cows that I started shaking hands with people one finger at a time." With the demands of the farm, Neef did not have a lot of time for school. Neef said of his education, "I managed to finish only the tenth grade, but everything I did was part of my education. I guess I always felt that education could come in a lot of ways. I didn't let schooling get in the way of my education through experience. Through experience, study, and association, we should learn something useful every day." Although, Neef would achieve great success in business, he had ordinary beginnings. Neef said of his early years, "From my youth, I felt that I was homely, awkward, and born to lose. Start with what you do well and improve from there."

During the depression, Neef worked at a sawmill. His job was to stack the newly cut lumber into piles. During this time he also started a little farm. He bought the rights to a homestead in Vale, Oregon with his brother Golden for forty dollars and began clearing the thirty acres with hoes, axes, and shovels on nights and weekends. They eventually started a company called Grigg Brothers Produce Company and started selling their garden produce door to door. Gradually, they got bigger and braver and began selling corn and potatoes store to store. To expand the number of stores available to purchase their produce, they developed a system of icing the corn and shipping it across the country. With their system, corn from Oregon could arrive fresh in New York in just seven days.

The Grigg brothers saw huge potential in the future of frozen food so when a flash freezing plant went bankrupt, Neef showed up for the auction and before he knew it he had the winning bid at $500,000. The Grigg brothers had expected the plant to sell for $250,000. The bid required 25 percent down so Neef and Golden mortgaged their homes and contacted all the lawyers and doctors they knew to raise $125,000. Neef said of buying the plant in Ontario, Oregon, "We didn't have much to put in it but some seasonal corn. We got by on that for a couple of years, and then in 1948 we started freezing potatoes."

Everybody thought Neef was crazy for freezing potatoes since they were available all year around. When Neef first began trying to sell frozen potatoes to restaurants and institutions they would say, "You're crazy. We can get a raw potato anytime we want it."

Neef would tell potential customers, "We can control the quality and offer you convenience," and then rather than argue with them, he would leave a box with them and say, "If you get too busy to peel your own, maybe you could try these." When they discovered the quality and convenience of frozen potatoes they were hooked. This was the beginning of the expansion of the frozen french fry.

They named their frozen food business Ore-Ida, which was officially founded in 1952 and began providing french fries and other produce across the country. In 1953, Ore-Ida produced a new product from the unusable shavings created while making french fries. Neef and his brother Golden were determined to figure out a more productive use for the leftover potato shavings since they had been selling them at a very low price as feed for livestock. They created bite-sized treats from the slivers of potato and called them Tater Tots®.

To introduce the new product, Neef took fifteen pounds of Tater Tots to the National Potato Convention. Neef bribed a chef at the convention to serve the bite-sized treats. They were very well received, and orders for the new product began to roll in. By 1960, Ore-Ida was producing 350 million pounds of finished product. Demand was exceeding their capacity, so a new potato-processing plant was opened in 1961 in Burley, Idaho.

In 1961, Ore-Ida made the transition from a private company to a public company to ensure the funds for company growth. Stock was sold to approximately 3,500 investors. The two hundred thousand shares of stock were issued by Kidder, Peabody and Company, a prominent security firm, for $13.50 a share. Demand for the stock raised it to $18 a share within the first hours of trading. Neef flew to New York to pick up a check for $2.48 million for the shares of Ore-Ida that were sold.

Ore-Ida continued to grow rapidly each year, and in 1964, they had sales of $31 million. Ore-Ida continued to expand to meet demand, and in 1965, sales exceeded $100 million. The Heinz Company was very interested in Ore-Ida and purchased the company for $30 million in 1965, and Ore-Ida became a wholly owned subsidiary of Heinz. Neef continued to serve as president. The company continued to grow, and by 1984, Ore-Ida had annual sales exceeding $350 million.

Neef said of the years of hard work, "It seemed to some that all at once we went from nothing to a major operation with over 3,000 employees. But actually, it took decades." Neef spent two decades farming and developing new delivery and processing methods before Ore-Ida was formed in 1952. It took another decade of work to acquire the means to expand nationwide.

Neef had a clear vision of what he could do, even when everyone else thought it impossible. Neef recalled, "I remember talking once to a newspaper editor of the *Ontario Observer*. At that time, no one had shipped frozen potatoes in carload lots. But I told him, 'I can visualize shipping ten carloads of frozen potatoes next year.' He laughed and said, 'Well, there's one thing I can say about you, you're a dreamer.' That next year we shipped hundreds of carloads of frozen potatoes." As the result of his vision, determination, and hard work, Neef was able to achieve his dreams and bless the lives of thousands.

> "In reflection it appears that any successes I've had or seen has been the result of a good idea, bolstered by determination and hard work."
>
> -Neef Grigg

Bill Child—A Dream and Forty Years of Work

"At age 22, Bill had taken over his father-in-law's retail appliance store, a 600-square foot cinder-block building on the edge of a cornfield in remote Syracuse, Utah. At the time the business was in debt, and its only asset was a three-quarter ton pickup truck used for home deliveries. . . . On the flip side, the company had a loyal customer base and a stellar reputation. With some financial discipline and sustained hard work, Bill was convinced the company could turn a profit."[82]

Bill had recently graduated with a teaching degree and had a good job offer when his father-in-law, RC Willey, died unexpectedly. Bill had been working with RC while going to school and was now needed to manage the business. Bill put his teaching career on hold and focused on the business. The business needed some operating cash, so Bill went to a bank to request a loan. His request was denied, and he was told he should close or sell the business. If Bill had listened to the experts, his business career would have been over. Bill had no business experience, but he did have a dream and the willingness to work. Even though Bill was confident that one day R.C. Willey would be a successful company, at times, thoughts of quitting entered his mind as he worked hard for many years with no profits.

It definitely was not easy. "It required him to get his hands dirty and work a lot of twelve-hour days."[83] He worked hard just to pay back the business debt he inherited. It took four years to pay off a $9,000 loan RC had taken to build a small warehouse. Bill minimized future loans and was thrifty in his personal and business life to avoid the burden and bondage of debt.

In 1965, after eleven years of working each day to grow the business, the store hit the sales milestone of $25,000 in a single day. It was an additional fifteen years of work to grow the annual sales of the company to $1 million. "By 2000, it wasn't unusual for the company to hit $18 million in sales on a single holiday. It's easy to gloss over the years of hard work that preceded this kind of success. For example, in forty years, Bill missed only two days of work due to an illness—in 1968 when he was down with the flu. Other than that, he showed up every day unless he was taking his annual family vacation."[84]

"In order to guarantee success, the willingness to work hard must be coupled with patience. Success doesn't happen overnight."[85] After forty years of hard work, persistence, and adherence to time-tested principles, Bill had taken the company to over $250 million a year in sales with no mortgages. On May 29, 1995, Bill Child sold his business to Warren Buffet for $175 million in Berkshire Hathaway stock. Bill followed the formula to achieve great success—a steady and long-term commitment to hard work and the adherence to true principles.

Steve Kerr—181 Pounds of Hard Work

"With his frail-looking frame, freckled face and milky skin, Kerr can walk onto any playground in the country with no chance of being picked first."[86] Steve Kerr was not highly recruited out of high school because he lacked speed and jumping ability, but what Steve Kerr lacked in physical ability he made up with hard work. Steve Kerr out-practiced others until he became one of the best shooters in basketball. He practiced hours each day shooting "five hundred free throws a day."[87] "His signature shooting style—quick jump, arm and fingers fully extended, hair flying—is one born of a million practice shots."[88] His hard work paid off with a fifteen-year career in the NBA, resulting in five NBA championships. Steve Kerr holds the NBA record for the best three-point shooting percentage in a season (52.4 percent in 1994–95) and retired from the NBA as the all-time leader in three-point shooting percentage for a career (45.4 percent).

Paul Allen and Bill Gates—Founders of Microsoft

"The creative path is rocky, with the risk of failure ever present and no guarantees. But even with its detours and blind alleys, it's the only road that I find fulfilling."

–Paul Allen

Paul Allen and Bill Gates attended Lakeside School together in Seattle, Washington. Although Allen was nearly three years older than Gates, they became friends as they both shared a passion for computers and programming.

Gates wrote of his early work on computers, "I had to take care of my own computer-time bill. This is what drove me to the commercial side of the software business. A bunch of us, including Paul Allen, got entry-level software programming jobs. For high school students the pay was extraordinary—about $5,000 each summer, part in cash and the rest in computer time. We also worked out deals with a few companies whereby we could use computers for free if we'd locate problems in their software.... One of the reasons I was so determined to help develop the personal computer is that I wanted one for myself."[89]

Allen and Gates watched as computer technology evolved and improved. With Intel's development of the new microprocessors, they saw that the day would soon come when there would be "a computer on every desk and in every home."[90] They saw a huge opportunity emerging. Gates wrote, "It seemed to us people would find all kinds of new uses for computing if it was cheap. Then, software would be the key to delivering the full potential of these machines."[91] Gates and Allen looked for ways they could develop software and utilize the new microprocessors.

Allen graduated from Lakeside School in 1971 and enrolled at Washington State University in Pullman, Washington. Gates made many bus trips across the state from Seattle to Pullman to work on various ideas with Allen. In 1972, they created a machine that read the data from roadway traffic counters and created reports. They established a business around this machine called Traf-O-Data. Gates wrote of this business, "Our prototype worked well, and we envisioned selling lots of our new machines across the country. We used it to process traffic-volume tapes for a few customers, but no one actually wanted to buy the machine. . . . Despite our disappointment, we still believed our future."[92]

In 1973, Gates enrolled at Harvard University in Cambridge, Massachusetts. Gates coaxed Allen to join him in Massachusetts. Allen left Washington State University to take a programming job for Honeywell in Boston. The two were again only a few miles apart. Gates wrote, "He drove over to Cambridge a lot so we could continue our long talks about future schemes."[93]

Gates and Allen sent letters from Gates's dorm room to all the big computer companies, offering to write software for them, but received no responses. By December 1974, they "were pretty discouraged"[94] when Allen showed Gates a copy of the January 1975 issue of *Popular Electronics*. The cover had a picture of the Altair 8800 with the headline, "World's First Minicomputer Kit to Rival Commercial Models."

The Altair 8800 did not contain software, so it was more of a novelty than a tool, but it did contain the new Intel 8080 microprocessor chip, and Gates and Allen saw an opportunity to create the needed software. Gates wrote, "I wanted to be involved from the beginning. The chance to get in on the first stages of the PC revolution seemed the opportunity of a lifetime."[95]

Gates and Allen sent a letter to the creator of the Altair, Ed Roberts, in New Mexico stating that they had software for his computer. Allen shared the following about contacting Roberts: "When we didn't hear back, we followed up with a phone call. 'You should talk to them. You're older,' Bill said. 'No you should do it, you're better at this kind of thing,' I said. We compromised. Bill would make the call but would say he was me. . . . 'This is Paul Allen in Boston,' Bill said. 'We've got a BASIC for the Altair that's just about finished, and we'd like to come out and show it to you.' I admired Bill's bravado but worried that he'd gone too far, since we'd yet to write the first line of code.

"Roberts was interested, but he was getting ten calls a day from people with similar claims. He told Bill what he'd told everyone else: The first person to walk through the door in Albuquerque with a BASIC that worked would get a contract for Altair."[96]

Gates and Allen began immediately to work on creating the promised software, Altair BASIC. The task before them was very difficult as they had to squeeze a lot of capability into the computer's small memory. The project was further complicated as they had only seen the Altair 8800 in pictures. Allen obtained a manual on the Intel 8080 chip and wrote a program that made the big computer at Harvard mimic the little Altair.

Gates wrote, "Writing good software requires a lot of concentration and writing BASIC for the Altair was exhausting. . . . Paul and I didn't sleep much and lost track of night and day. When I did fall asleep, it was often at my desk or on the floor. Some days I didn't eat or see anyone. But after five weeks, our BASIC was written."[97]

"Allen flew to New Mexico, never having tested the program on an actual Altair and not knowing for sure if it would work. Arriving at the headquarters of Roberts' company . . ., he saw an Altair for the first time. Allen nervously entered the language program onto the machine as Roberts watched. . . . After absorbing the instructions, the Altair responded: the teletype in front of Allen asked him a question about the specifications. He answered, and then it typed, 'Ready.' With that word, a new software industry was launched. Roberts decided on the spot to offer the new BASIC with his computers."[98]

On April 4, 1975, Gates and Allen established a company called Micro-soft (the hyphen was later removed). Gates wrote, "We knew getting a company started would mean sacrifice. But we also realized we had to do it then or forever lose the opportunity to make it in microcomputer software. . . . Paul quit his programming job, and I decided to go on leave from Harvard."[99]

Microsoft signed an agreement with Roberts for his company to pay a royalty for each copy of Altair BASIC sold. In the first year, the agreement generated $16,000 in revenue for Microsoft and was the first of many licensing agreements signed by Microsoft for the use of its software.

Gates and Allen worked at a rigorous pace to build their company. Gates "often worked at his desk from 9:30 am to midnight, fueled by delivered pizza and caffeinated drinks."[100] Allen wrote of the days building Microsoft, "We would just work until we dropped. . . . Even with the absurd hours . . . we were still having the times of our lives. . . . It's hard to explain to people how much fun it was."[101]

Their vision and hard work paid off, generating billions in profits. They exceeded even their loftiest expectations. Allen wrote, "One time I asked Bill, 'If everything went right, how big do you think our company could be?' He said, 'I think we could get it up to thirty-five programmers.' That sounded really ambitious to me."[102] Today

Microsoft has a few more than thirty-five programmers with a total of 97,000 employees and over $73 billion in revenue.

In 1995, Bill Gates wrote, "People often ask me to explain Microsoft's success. They want to know the secret of getting from a two-man, shoestring operation to a company with 17,000 employees and more than $6 billion a year in sales. Of course, there is no simple answer . . . but I think the most important element was our original vision."

Paul Allen summed up the reason for his success saying, "My really big ideas have all begun with . . . a few basic questions: Where is the leading edge of discovery headed? What should exist but doesn't yet? How can I create something to help meet the need, and who might be enlisted to join the crusade?"[103]

CAMERON C. TAYLOR

CHAPTER VI
LESSONS LEARNED FROM ROGER BANNISTER

"We enjoy struggling to get the best out of ourselves. . .
Struggles give us deep satisfaction, perhaps the most
real satisfaction we ever have in life."

-Roger Bannister

Roger Bannister participated in his first cross-country race when he was eleven years old. He began the race at a very fast pace and was determined that he was going to win. He had not trained, and with extreme pain and exhaustion, he finished in eighteenth place. The next year, he decided to train for this cross-country race. No one his age had ever won, but Bannister felt, with proper training, he could win. His training consisted of running two and a half miles as fast as he could twice a week and then taking two days to recover. As the race neared commencement, Bannister watched the race favorite, who to him, appeared to be a giant. Bannister was certain he was more prepared for the race than the favorite. Bannister wrote of this race, "I won the race, and remember with pleasure the utter astonishment of all my school friends."[104] Bannister also won the race the next two years. He recognized that training was the key to his success saying, "I worked furiously.... It wasn't easy to win.... I was not a better runner than the others, in the sense of having more innate ability."[105] In the next two years, Bannister took no interest in organized running.

Bannister went to Oxford in the fall of 1946 to study medicine. Bannister wrote, "In Oxford, I had been told, a man without a sport is like a ship without a sail. Here it seemed, you could both work and play, each being complementary to the other. The idea appealed to me, the only question being to decide which sport to take up.... I decided to devote a proportion of my time ... to making myself a good runner."[106]

Bannister made a visit to the university track for a run and persuaded a well-built oarsman to come with him. After about thirty minutes running around the track, the groundsman approached and began talking of the great runners he had seen at Oxford. He looked at the oarsman and said, "I think you might become a runner."[107] The groundsman then turned to Bannister and said, "I'm afraid that you'll never be any good. You just haven't got the strength or the build for it."[108]

Bannister did not let this assessment discourage him and decided to run the mile in a sporting event for freshman taking place in two weeks. He began training using a similar pattern from his earlier cross-country events. Bannister finished second in the competition with a time of 4 minutes and 53 seconds.

Bannister began to focus on the mile race and earned a spot on the team. On March 22, 1947, in a meet against Cambridge, Bannister secured his first victory in the mile with a time of 4 minutes and 30.8 seconds. Bannister wrote of this race, "I was only third string, and my orders were to move into the lead if the Cambridge runners failed to set the right pace. . . . When the gun fired, the Cambridge runners shot into the lead so I stayed back at a respectful distance. . . . I was as tired as everyone else, but suddenly for the first time I felt a crazy desire to overtake the whole field. I raced through into the lead, and a feeling of great mental and physical excitement swept over me. I forgot my tiredness. I suddenly tapped that hidden source of energy I always suspected I possessed. I won by twenty yards."[109]

Bannister recognized that if he wanted to see improvement in his running, it would require continuous self-discipline. Bannister's time dedicated to running was limited, but he consistently ran three or four times a week for about thirty minutes and worked his way from third string to the leader of the first team.

By the end of 1947, Bannister was considered as a candidate for the 1948 Olympic Games. Bannister did not feel he was yet ready for competition at this level and did not want to jeopardize his bid for the 1952 Olympic Games.

In 1948, Bannister entered the A.A.A. Championship, which was the highest level of competition he had faced to date. He finished in fourth place with a time of 4 minutes and 17.2 seconds, his fastest to date.

Bannister attended the 1948 Olympics as a spectator and quickly realized that the times that enabled him to win at Oxford meets would not be good enough to compete with the world's top athletes. With his sights on the 1952 Olympics, he knew he had to set new goals and create a more vigorous training program.

In 1949, Oxford had arranged for athletic matches with the Ivy League schools in America. Bannister was excited for his races in America and trained hard in the summer with a plan to reach his peak for the Ivy League matches.

On June 11, 1949, Princeton's Palmer Stadium was the host of an international track meet, pitting the top athletes from Oxford and Cambridge with the stars of Princeton and Cornell. The marquee race was the mile, which featured the Princeton captain, Ron Wittreich, who was one of America's top milers, and Roger Bannister, the Oxford captain, who was one of England's top milers. Bannister took the lead near the end of the third lap and finished in first place with a new personal best time of 4 minutes and 11.1 seconds and the second fastest mile in America that year.

Following the athletic matches in America, Bannister stayed for six weeks with family and friends in New York. During this time, he did not train and kept very irregular hours and had hoped he would not have to compete for the remainder of the year. Shortly after arriving home in England, he was asked to compete and told that there was great excitement following his races in America, and it would be a great disappointment if he did not compete. Bannister accepted the invite but knew he was not in proper shape for a race.

Bannister wrote of this race, "An athlete has no right to run if he is not fit—even though he may be to blame for having stopped his training. I could not rise to the challenge and crawled home in third place. This was the first race in my life in which I had so decidedly failed to do what was expected of me. I felt very humbled. . . . As I left the stadium the news of my defeat was already headlined in the evening paper, 'Bannister Fails in Mile.' . . . After this experience I felt that no athlete is justified in running when inadequately trained."[110]

In 1950, at a race in New Zealand, Bannister improved his mile time to 4 minutes and 9.9 seconds, and in the A.A.A. Championships on July 14, 1951, Bannister ran a new personal best mile in 4 minutes and 7.8 seconds. In the winter of 1951, Bannister began his plan for the 1952 Olympics. The early ranking for the Olympic Games had Bannister projected at fourth place, but Bannister had his eyes on the gold. Bannister wrote, "An Olympic victory is an honor that may come only once to a nation; for me to achieve it, I must have an absolutely single aim. . . . I decided that it was my duty to train as I thought best for the Olympic final, whatever that might involve. It was a goal so high as to be worth every sacrifice. No compromise was possible."[111]

Ten days before the Olympic final, Bannister ran his final time trial. He completed the ¾ mile in 2 minutes and 52.9 seconds, which was nearly four seconds faster than the world record. Bannister wrote, "I never imagined I could run as fast as this. . . . I felt now that in [the Olympic] final race, with a day's rest after the heat, I could beat even the world record [and] should be fast enough to win. . . . [The] next morning I opened the paper and saw the headlines, 'Semi-finals for the Olympic 1,500 meter.' There had never been semi-finals before. It was crazy for such an exhausting distance. . . . I felt the victim of circumstance, because I knew the change would hit me harder than the other competitors."[112]

Bannister qualified for the finals, but he felt the strain from the previous two races in two days, writing, "I had hardly the strength to warm up. As I walked out in front of those 70,000 spectators, my step had no spring, my face no color. . . . There was too little time between the races to regain my strength."[113]

Bannister was in second prior to the final bend and was in position for his final effort. Bannister wrote, "This was the crucial moment, for which I had waited so long. But my legs were aching and I had no strength left to force them faster. I had a sickening feeling of exhaustion and powerlessness as Barthel came past me, chased by McMillen. . . . I came in fourth, and a few yards covered the first six. The first eight of us had broken the previous Olympic record [set] in 1936. . . . I found new meaning in the Olympic words that the important thing was not the winning but the taking part—not the conquering but the fighting well."[114]

With the Olympics over, Bannister needed a new focus. Bannister wrote, "Everyone has to give up something for the sake of his sport. To justify my sacrifices I had to have some goal." The goal that energized Bannister to move on from the Olympics was the four-minute mile. Bannister described his intensified training: "[I] would . . . run as many as ten quarter-miles, each in about 63 seconds, and with an interval of two to three minutes between each. This was much more strenuous training than I had ever done before. It left me exhausted . . . but it could be accomplished within the half-hour a day that I was able to spare for training."[115]

In December 1952, John Landy of Australia shocked the world by running the fastest mile since the world record in 1945 with a time of

4 minutes and 2.1 seconds. Landy had also made the four-minute mile his goal. Bannister wrote, "The four-minute mile had become rather like an Everest—a challenge to the human spirit. It was a barrier that seemed to defy all attempts to break it."[116]

Landy trained harder than any other distance runner in the world. His program consisted of weight lifting and running every day to a total of two hundred miles a month. "By April 1954 Landy had won six races all in times less than 4 minutes 3 seconds, a record achieved by no other athlete in history."[117] While Landy had achieved unprecedented success in the mile, after each race there were headlines that read, "Landy Fails" since he had come up short of the 4-minute mile. After one race, Landy said of the four-minute mile, "It's a brick wall. I shall not attempt it again."

Bannister continued his training of ten consecutive quarter miles working to reduce the time of each quarter to the target of 60 seconds. He had gotten each quarter to a time of 61 seconds, but no matter how hard he tried, "it did not seem possible to reach . . . 60 seconds."[118]

Bannister decided to take a break from training to do a few days of camping and climbing. After a three-day break, he was able to run the quarter miles in 59 seconds each. The Oxford A.A.A. race was less than three weeks away and would be Bannister's first race in eight months, and he felt that he had reached his peak physically and psychologically.[119]

Excitement leading up to the race was intensifying with hopes of seeing a four-minute mile. Could Bannister break the barrier or would it be another failed attempt? In the week prior to the race, Bannister ran the race in his mind each night. When he visualized himself at the starting line, his body would grow nervous and begin to tremble. Bannister would calm himself down and run the race in his mind.

The day of May 6, 1954 arrived, and the four-minute mile attempt was on. Bannister described the race, "At three-quarters the time was 3 minutes and .7 seconds, and by now the crowd was roaring. Somehow I had to run that last lap in 59 seconds. . . . I had a moment of mixed joy and anguish, when my mind took over. It raced well ahead of my body and drew my body compellingly forward. I felt that the moment of a lifetime had come. . . . I drove on. . . . The noise in my ears was that of the faithful Oxford crowd. Their hope and encouragement gave me greater strength. I had now turned the last bend and there were only fifty yards more. My body had long since exhausted all its energy, but it went on running just the same. The physical overdraft came only from greater willpower. This was the crucial moment when my legs were strong enough to carry me over the last few yards as they could never have done in previous years. . . . I leapt at the tape. . . . My effort was over and I collapsed almost unconscious. . . . It was only then that real pain overtook me. I felt like an exploded flashlight with no will to live. . . . I knew I had done it before I heard the time. . . . The stop-watches held the answer. The announcement came—'Result of the one mile . . . time 3 minutes'—the rest lost in the roar of excitement. . . . I . . . scampered around the track in a burst of spontaneous joy. . . . In the wonderful joy my pain was forgotten and I wanted to prolong those precious moments of realization."[120]

Lesson One: Instead of saying "That's Impossible" ask the question "How is it Possible?"

"Our success on the track was only a very small part of our lives, but we hoped it had taught us a discipline that was transferable to other spheres."

– Roger Bannister

In 1952, Roger Bannister set the goal to be the first man to run a mile in under 4 minutes and intensified his training. The record for the mile run remained at 4 minutes and 1.4 seconds for nine years. "For years, the four-minute mile was considered not merely unreachable but, according to physiologists of the time, dangerous to the health of any athlete who attempted to reach it."[121] On May 6, 1954, Roger Bannister ran the mile in 3 minutes and 59.4 seconds, setting a new world record and breaking the proclaimed "impossible" barrier. In an interview, Bannister said, "There was a mystique, a belief that it couldn't be done, but I think it was more of a psychological barrier than a physical barrier."[122]

Once Roger Bannister removed this psychological barrier, the door was opened for others to achieve this feat. On June 21, 1954, just forty-six days after Bannister had set this record, John Landy broke Bannister's record in Turku, Finland, and today there are hundreds of people who have run a mile in under four minutes.

Many people have been conditioned with thoughts of what can't be done. Studies have shown that within the first eighteen years of our lives, the average person is told "no" more than 148,000 times.[123] We are constantly being told by parents, friends, teachers, television, and co-workers what we cannot do. This conditioning causes many of us to achieve a small fraction of our potential and results in a pessimistic approach to life. A pessimist approaches life with statements of what can't be done instead of asking how it can be done.

To dispel the pessimist in each of us, we must transform our approach to life by finding solutions instead of excuses. Instead of saying, "I can't do it," we should find a solution that begins by asking the question, "How can I do it?" Instead of saying "I can't afford it," or "It's impossible," begin asking the questions, "How can I afford it?" and "How is it possible?" This small change in our approach to life will produce great outcomes. Elbert Hubbard wrote, "The world is moving so fast these days that the man who says it can't be done is generally interrupted by someone doing it."

Lesson 2: We should not ask the question, "How am I doing compared to so and so?" We should ask, "Am I doing my personal best?"

The only two men in the world to have broken the four-minute barrier were set to compete against each other on August 7, 1954, just six weeks after John Landy had broken Roger Bannister's four-minute mile world record. The event took place at the Empire Games in Vancouver, BC. The race was billed as "The Miracle Mile," and 35,000 filled Empire Stadium and hundreds of thousands listened on the radio and watched on television. Bannister said of this race, "Landy and I were the only two runners to have broken the four-minute mile, and we were both at the peak of our training. There had never been a race like this. . . . The stadium was filled with one of the most enthusiastic crowds I have ever seen. The setting was perfect."[124]

Landy took an early lead and led for most of the race. He had built a ten-yard lead by the third lap but was overtaken on the last bend by Bannister, who won the race with a time of 3 minutes 58.8 seconds. Landy also finished in less than 4 minutes, just 0.8 seconds behind Bannister. The crucial moment of the race occurred when Landy looked back over his left shoulder to see where Bannister was, and Bannister burst past him on the right to take the lead and the victory. This moment in the race was captured by photographer Charlie Warner and was later turned into a life-size bronze sculpted by Jack Harman in 1967. This sculpture stood for many years at the entrance to Empire Stadium and was eventually moved to the Pacific National Exhibition fairgrounds. When asked about the statue, Landy said, "While Lot's wife was turned into a pillar of salt for looking back, I am probably the only one ever turned into bronze for looking back."

When we spend time comparing our lives to others, it can distract us from doing our personal best. Life is not a competition with others. Life is a competition with yourself—to do your personal best each day.

Lesson 3: It is by pushing ourselves to our current maximum that we open the door of growth to a new maximum.

The world record in the mile has been broken eighteen times since Roger Bannister's world record in 1954. The current record holder is

Hicham El Guerrouj at a time of 3 minutes and 43.13 seconds, set in 1999. The record time for the mile fell an average of .36 seconds each year. Bannister wrote of these improvements saying, "The main reason for the steady improvement lies in the training—more than two hours each day, often in two hour sessions, instead of my daily 30 minutes."[125]

It is by pushing ourselves to our current maximum that we open the door of growth to a new maximum. For example, much of the growth from weightlifting comes from the final reps before you can lift no more. If you could bench press two hundred pounds a maximum of ten reps, 80 percent of muscle growth and increased strength will result from the final two reps, and 20 percent of the growth results from the first eight reps. The last two reps are the hardest, but if neglected, will cost you 80 percent of your growth. It does not require twice the effort to achieve twice the improvement, because the final efforts of maximum exertion result in exponential returns. Roger Bannister wrote, "The man who can drive himself further once the effort gets painful is the man who will win."

ATTRIBUTE 13
GRATEFUL

"Gratitude is not only the greatest of virtues, but the parent of all others."

-CICERO

CHAPTER VII
THE JOY OF GRATITUDE

"Nothing will diminish your life more
quickly and profoundly than being ungrateful.
Conversely, nothing will enlarge your life more
quickly and dramatically than gratitude."

-Don Soderquist

"Do you want to know the cure for anger, bitterness, resentment, jealousy, low self-esteem, a quarreling spirit, and other modern maladies? Do you want to live a better life? It's really simple. Be grateful for what you have."[126]

Thank-You Notes

"I can live for two months on a good compliment."

-Mark Twain

Each week on the TV show *Late Night with Jimmy Fallon*, Fallon takes time to write humorous thank-you notes such as:

- "Thank you, aliens, for being advanced enough to have spaceships, but not advanced enough to wear pants."
- "Thank you to the phrase 'the greatest thing since sliced bread' for making me seriously think about who is in charge of deciding what the greatest thing is."
- "Thank you, dolls, for always being one missing eye away from being the creepiest thing ever."
- "Thank you, geometry, for proving that boredom comes in all shapes and sizes."
- "Thank you, 15-pound baby born in England, which sounds even more impressive when you realize that's like 30 American dollars."
- "Thank you, giant Easter bunny outfits, for being the most fun and festive way to creep people out."
- "Thank you, oven mitts, or as I call you—blind puppets."

While most of us will never write thank-you notes like Jimmy Fallon, a handwritten thank-you note is a great way to express appreciation and give thanks. Just as Jimmy Fallon writes thank-you notes on his show each Friday, we should each pick a day each week to write a few thank-you notes to our family, friends, coworkers, clients, etc.

In each of my companies, we send many handwritten thank-you

notes each week. For example, each of my directors of education sends a thank-you note and gift to the meeting planner we worked with following an event, and our director of legal services sends a gift and handwritten thank-you note to each new client.

As I was writing this chapter, my wife brought in the mail for the day. In the mail was a handwritten thank-you note to my wife and me from a friend. The note reads in part:

"You guys seriously are fantastic examples of friendship—to the entire community. What a blessing you have been in our lives, and I'm sure you are proving to be a great blessing to Rigby, Idaho. We love the Taylors. . . . I have looked up to you and your family ever since we met. Thanks for your great example of righteousness and hard work."

This letter from my friend is a great example of a powerful thank-you note. Receiving a note like this provides me with a tremendous lift and fills me with a desire to do even better. This note will be placed in a file I keep with all the positive notes I have received from family, friends, book readers, seminar attendees, employees, etc. Whenever I feel down, I will pull out this file and read through these notes, and I am energized and my spirits are quickly raised. As I put this most recent note in the file, I read through other notes I had saved. I thought I would share a few as examples of thank-you letters that have lifted me.

Handwritten thank-you note from an executive at one of my publishers: "Your books have been a greater influence on me than all the others we've published. I can't thank you enough for all you've taught me and the opportunity to have you as one of our authors."

Handwritten thank-you note from a friend and former employee: "I can't thank you enough for the amazing principles you have exemplified for me, and for all you've done! You guys are my heroes, and I hope to be like you! We love you."

Handwritten note from a nine year old on one of the football teams I coached: "Thank you for coaching my team. You are the best coach. I wish you would be our coach next year too."

Note from my wife: "Thank you for being such an incredible husband and father. You have always put us first in your life, and I'm so grateful for the example you are for our children. I hope that Mitchell and Enoch will follow in your footsteps and that Kennedy will search for a spouse that is like her dad. I am thankful for your leadership in our home. Your patience, your kindness, and your willingness to serve all around you bring blessings to our home, and for that, I am grateful. I am thankful for your constant desire to learn and grow. You are an example to me of seeking diligently out of the best books. Our family and the lives of thousands have been improved because of your willingness to learn and to teach others what you have learned. You really are a gifted teacher. You have a way of taking concepts and teaching them in a way that is understandable. You are quick to listen, and you try to understand others instead of snapping to a judgment, and you are kind to those who really don't deserve your patience or kindness. I love and admire you. I think it is a blessing to know you, so the fact that I am married to you makes me feel 'blessed above all women.' I love you, sweetheart. Thank you for loving me so well."

If you do not have a thank-you note file, start one today. If you are not in the habit of giving handwritten thank-you notes, begin today so others can place them in their thank-you note file and read them again and again. A verbal thank you and expression of appreciation is fantastic, but a written note can be read again and again and lift a person for years to come.

Gratitude Journal

You can keep a copy of the thank-you notes you give and receive with your gratitude journal. Keeping a book of thanks is a great way to cultivate and maintain the attribute of gratitude. Journals are a way of counting our blessings and create an inventory of these blessings for you to review and remember.

Lou Gehrig—The Luckiest Man

Lou Gehrig played first base for the New York Yankees and earned the nickname "The Iron Horse" for his durability and ability to play even when sick or injured. He set the Major League record for most consecutive games played (2,130 games) without a miss over a fourteen-year period from 1925 to 1939. He is considered one of the greatest players of all times with a career batting average of .340, three Triple Crown titles, and six World Series titles.

In 1939, Gehrig felt weak and had a hard time running, hitting, and fielding. He even fell down in the clubhouse while getting dressed. He was unsure what the trouble was, but he pulled himself from the lineup for the benefit of the team. On his thirty-sixth birthday, June 19, 1939, Gehrig learned that he was dying from an illness that affects the central nervous system called amyotrophic lateral sclerosis—now commonly called Lou Gehrig disease. Gehrig would not play another game for the Yankees and retired from baseball. The team and fans wanted to let Gehrig know how deeply they cared about him, so they organized a Lou Gehrig Appreciation Day at Yankee Stadium on July 4, 1939.

Gehrig was presented many gifts, commemorative plaques, and trophies, and when it was Gehrig's turn to address the crowd, he was overcome with emotion. The master of ceremonies announced, "Ladies and gentlemen, Lou Gehrig has asked me to thank you all for him. He is too moved to speak." In response the crowd began to chant, "We want Lou! We want Lou!" Gehrig wiped his eyes and blew his nose and walked to the microphone. He began, "Fans, for the past two weeks you have been reading about a bad break I got. Yet today, I consider myself the luckiest man on the face of the earth."

"It was a courageous speech. Lou didn't complain about his terrible illness. Instead he spoke of his many blessings and of the future. 'Sure, I'm lucky,' he said when he spoke of his years in baseball. 'Sure, I'm lucky,' he said again when he spoke of his fans and family. Lou spoke about how good people had been to him. He praised his teammates. He thanked his parents and his wife, whom he called a tower of strength."[127]

Gehrig ended his speech saying, "So I close in saying that I might have had a bad break, but I have an awful lot to live for. Thank you." The crowd gave Gehrig a standing ovation for nearly two minutes. Gehrig wiped tears from his face with a handkerchief as he stepped away from the microphone. The band began to play "I Love You Truly," and the crowd began to chant, "We love you, Lou." As the music played and the fans chatted, Babe Ruth gave Gehrig a big hug. Gehrig set an example of how to live even when faced with death. Gehrig passed away on June 2, 1941, at the age of thirty-seven.

Corrie and Betsie ten Boom—Give Thanks in All Circumstances

In 1944, Corrie and Betsie ten Boom were arrested by the Nazis for harboring Jews in their home. They were taken to the Scheveningen prison and later transferred to Ravensbrück Concentration Camp in northern Germany. They were known as Prisoner 66729 and Prisoner 66730 and were never called by name. When they arrived at Ravensbrück, they were assigned to Barrack 28. As they entered the barracks, they had to fight back the urge to vomit from the foul smells. There were no beds, but wooden shelves that were three platforms high, which filled the room. They followed the guard in a single-file line down very narrow aisles. The sleeping shelves were built so closely together that you could not sit up without hitting your head on the shelf above. The newly arrived prisoners crowded into their assigned area with feelings of claustrophobia. As Corrie entered the shelves, she felt a pinch on her leg. The area was infested with fleas. As Corrie was repeatedly bitten, she asked her sister, "How can we live in such a place?"

Her sister answered, "Give thanks in all circumstances. That's what we can do. We can start right now to thank God for every single thing about this new barracks."

Corrie looked around the dark and smelly room and asked, "Such as?"

Betsie answered, "Such as being assigned together." Betsie went on to name a number of other items to be thankful for and then continued, "Thank you for the fleas."

Corrie interrupted her, "The fleas! Betsie, there's no way even

God can make me grateful for a flea."

Betsie again quoted, "Give thanks in all circumstances. It doesn't say in pleasant circumstances. Fleas are part of this place." The two sisters stood between the bunks and gave thanks for fleas.

A few weeks later, Betsie overheard one of the guards refuse to enter the barracks because of all the fleas. They had been surprised by the lack of interference and abuse from the guards, and now she knew why. The fleas were a blessing that kept the guards away.[128]

Conclusion

"Researchers have measured physiological activity under various emotional conditions, and found that in a state of appreciation, good things happen to your mind, heart, and body: your heart rate slows, your blood pressure drops, and your digestion is facilitated. You feel more peaceful, your stress diminishes, and your immune system benefits."[129] There is joy in a life filled with gratitude.

ATTRIBUTE 14
SERVANT LEADER

"He that is greatest among you
shall be your servant."

-MATTHEW 23:11

CHAPTER VIII
THE 8 MOTIVES OF A HUMBLE LEADER

"We come nearest to the great when we are great in humility."

-Rabindranath Togare

The author of the book *Good to Great* conducted an extensive five-year research project to identify the factors that caused companies to move from good to great. One of the critical factors identified was the leadership of the company. Jim Collins wrote, "We were surprised, shocked really, to discover the type of leadership required for turning a good company into a great one. Compared to high-profile leaders with big personalities who make headlines and become celebrities, the good-to-great leaders seem to have come from Mars. Self-effacing, quiet, reserved, even shy—these leaders are a paradoxical blend of personal humility and professional will. They are more like Lincoln and Socrates than Patton or Caesar. . . . Their ambition is first and foremost for the institution, not themselves."[130]

Humble Leader vs. Pride-Driven Leader

The idea of servant leadership is difficult for many to grasp because it is opposite to much of the leadership that is modeled and taught in the world. The key to identifying and becoming a humble leader is to have the correct motives for our actions. It is often not the act but the motive for the act that reveals the true nature of a leader. To cultivate the attributes of a servant leader, we must understand the underlying motives that drive a humble leader and the contrasting motives of a pride-driven leader.

MOTIVES

HUMBLE LEADER	PRIDE-DRIVEN LEADER
1. Service	1. Position
2. Learn/Grow	2. Know-It-All
3. Gives Credit to Others	3. Takes Credit for Success
4. Do Your Personal Best	4. Be Better Than Others
5. Self-Confidence	5. Social Status
6. Mission	6. Money
7. Love	7. Power
8. Joy of Gratitude	8. Pain of Lack

1. Service vs. Position

Humble leaders desire to serve others. Pride-driven leaders are focused on titles and position so they can be served.

2. Learn/Grow vs. Know-It-All

Humble leaders are genuinely interested in what others have to say. They know they do not have all the answers and continually seek to learn from the insights and experiences of others—they "approach others with open minds and are willing to be taught."[131] Humble leaders listen more than they talk. Pride-driven leaders believe they know best and are more interested in talking about themselves than learning from others.

3. Gives Credit to Others vs. Takes Credit for Success

Humble leaders give credit for success to others and are not concerned with praise and adulation. Pride-driven leaders speak in a boastful or bragging manner of accomplishments in an attempt to impress others. Pride-driven leaders may even take credit for the accomplishments of others in their quest to receive attention and praise. Humble leaders will take responsibility when things go poorly while pride-driven leaders will find someone or something to blame.

4. Do Your Personal Best vs. Be Better Than Others

Walter Payton, one of the greatest running backs in NFL history, taught, "A winner is somebody who has given his best effort, who has tried the hardest they possibly can, who has utilized every ounce of energy and strength within them to accomplish something. It doesn't mean that they accomplished it or failed, it means that they've given it their best. That's a winner."[132]

A story from the life of Michael Jordan illustrates the focus on our performance instead of the performance of others. For three years in a row (1988-1990), Jordan and the Chicago Bulls were defeated in the Eastern Conference Finals by the Detroit Pistons. Some questioned whether the Bulls would ever make it to the NBA finals, and in an interview following another playoff defeat by the Detroit Pistons, Michael Jordan was asked why they could not beat the Detroit Pistons. Michael Jordan responded by saying that they could not worry about the Detroit Pistons. They just had to focus on improving their team and getting better so they could beat anyone. Michael Jordan and the Bulls went on to win six NBA titles over the next eight years. Michael Jordan wrote, "I've always believed that if you put in the work, the results will come. I don't do things half-heartedly. Because I know if I do, then I can expect half-hearted results."[133]

The legendary UCLA Coach John Wooden provides another powerful example. He wrote, "I never talked about winning or beating an opponent. In fact, I rarely mentioned the opponent's name. One player joked that just before games our manager would go to the lobby and buy a program in order to know who the team was playing that day. 'Let them worry about us,' was my philosophy. My job, and the team's job, was to get us as close to being as good as we could get."[134]

"In 1962, UCLA reached the Final Four for the first time ever. We did it with a group of young men Sports Illustrated described as having 'no height, no center, no muscle, no poise, no experience, no substitutes, and no chance.'"[135] UCLA lost seven of their first eleven games that year, but everyone "kept working hard and improving. . . . Their effort produced dramatic results as the season progressed, and UCLA won 14 of the final 18 games, became Pac-8 champions, and went to the NCAA tournament. In the regionals at Provo, Utah, the Bruins outscored Utah State and then Oregon State to advance to the Final Four. . . . This was quite a surprise to most basketball fans around the country. Our 72-70 loss in the last seconds of the Final Four semifinals to the defending and eventual champion, Cincinnati, provided great evidence of how one can 'lose' and still win. . . . Cincinnati's best was slightly better than ours. . . . The final score can never make you a loser when you've done your best. . . . What is success? For many it's trophies or blue ribbons. . . . But I don't measure it like that. The highest success is in your effort—giving it your personal best."[136]

One of John Wooden's most influential teachers was his dad. His dad taught him early and often, "Johnny, don't try to be better than somebody else, but never cease trying to be the best you can be."[137]

Humble leaders are not worried about how they are doing in relation to others and instead focus on doing their personal best. Humble leaders are cooperative, seek to lift others, and celebrate the success of others. Humble leaders have a very positive view of themselves and others but comparisons are not a part of their nature.

A pride-driven leader sees life as a competition—viewing others as opponents and enemies. They belittle the successes of others with the belief that the success of others detracts from their success. They continually measure their value, accomplishments, work, wealth, and talents in relation to others. Pride-driven leaders are more concerned that their income is more than the income of others than that it meets their needs. "Pride gets no pleasure out of having something, only out of having more of it than the next man. We say that people are proud of being rich, or clever, or good-looking, but they are not. They are proud of being richer, or cleverer, or better-looking than others.

If everyone else became equally rich, or clever, or good-looking there would be nothing to be proud about. It is the comparison that makes you proud: the pleasure of being above the rest. Once the element of competition has gone, pride has gone."[138] Pride-driven leaders seek to create hierarchies and class systems in which they are above others.

5. Self Confidence vs. Social Status

For humble leaders, self-confidence is their source of worth and respect and comes from within. Humble leaders seek the bounties of life they enjoy without a thought of what others think or say. They value freedom and independence and do not submit to the bondage of men's judgment.

For pride-driven leaders, social status is their source of worth and respect and comes from the outside. Pride-driven leaders focus on the bounties of life that the world says are the best or most important and are interested in the fame that comes with positions of leadership.

6. Mission vs. Money

Near the end of his life, Sam Walton, the founder of Walmart, said, "I have concentrated all along on building the finest retailing company that we possibly could. Period. Creating a huge personal fortune was never a goal of mine."[139] Humble leaders are driven by a mission to help others. They are concerned with building a company that contributes to and improves society. Their financial success is a by-product of their mission to help others. Pride-driven leaders are driven by money. Financial success is not a by-product of their mission but is their mission.

7. Love vs. Power

"If you want to test a man's character, give him power."
–Abraham Lincoln

Humble leaders are motivated by love. They lead by persuasion, gentleness, and long-suffering. Pride-driven leaders are motivated by power. They rule by control and force. C.S. Lewis wrote that "nothing makes a man feel superior to others as being able to move them about like toy soldiers."[140] "The proud man, even when he has got more than he can possibly want, will try to get still more just to assert his power. Nearly all those evils in the world which people put down to greed or selfishness are really far more the result of pride."[141] It is a misconception to think that the humble are doormats to the proud—the influence of the humble leader is far superior to the power of the pride-driven leader.

8. Joy of Gratitude vs. Pain of Lack

Humble leaders are filled with the joy of gratitude. Humble leaders focus on what they have, while pride-driven leaders focus on what they lack. Envy is a form of pride that focuses on what we do not have. "Envy is pained at what another person has and desires to spoil it. Envy is an urge to spoil or devalue what is good in another. Envy is born out of the pain of emptiness, of lack; the urge is to regain some internal balance by denigrating the goodness of the other. My cup is empty; I can't tolerate the fullness of yours, so I spoil it. Destructive envy represents an urgent need to spoil so as not to have to experience the pain of lack."[142]

A classic example of envy is found in the book of Genesis: "Now Israel loved Joseph more than all his children, because he was the son of his old age: and he made him a coat of many colors. And when his brethren saw that their father loved him more than all his brethren, they hated him."[143] To eliminate the pain of lack, his brothers "moved with envy, sold Joseph into Egypt."[144] Other common manifestations of envy are faultfinding, backbiting, and gossiping to pull down others.

Becoming a Servant Leader

To become a servant leader we must evaluate the motives for our actions and develop the attribute of humility. In the words of C.S. Lewis, "If anyone would like to acquire humility . . . the first step is to realize that one is proud. . . . If you think you are not conceited, it means you are very conceited indeed."[145]

George Washington—A Servant Leader

"I was but the humble agent of favoring Heaven. . . . My
first wish is . . . to see the whole world in peace, and the
inhabitants of it as one band of brothers, striving who
should contribute most to the happiness of mankind."
                                              -George Washington

George Washington was a key figure in the founding of the United States of America. Washington served as the leader of the Continental Army during the Revolutionary War. He presided over the Constitutional Convention, and he served as the country's first president. His leadership was vital to the success of each of these events. The following are a few stories and quotes from the life of Washington that provide a powerful example of a servant leader.

"In the year 1754, when about twenty-two years of age, [Washington] was stationed in Alexandria, as Colonel of a regiment of Virginia troops. During his stay in that town, an election for members of the House of Burgesses took place. The candidates were Colonel George Fairfax and a Mr. Elzey. His warm friendship for Colonel Fairfax brought him in collision with a Mr. Payne, the friend of Mr. Elzey. In consequence of some offensive language into which he was betrayed towards Mr. Payne, that individual struck him with a stick, and so violent was the blow, that it knocked him down.

"There being a great excitement among the officers and men belonging to his regiment because of this indignity offered their beloved commander, he forthwith employed his influence in allaying the tumult, and then retired to his lodgings in a public house. From thence he wrote a note to Mr. Payne, requesting that he would meet him next morning at the tavern as he wished to see him in reference to their recent disagreement. Payne, in expectation of an unpleasant interview, repaired accordingly to the appointed place, and instead of a hostile meeting, found Washington prepared to acknowledge his fault, and solicit pardon for the offence given in an unguarded moment. It is needless to say, that Payne witnessed with admiration, this triumph of principle over passion, and that a friendship was kindled in his bosom, which he did not cease to cherish as long as he lived."[146]

The following year in 1755, during the French and Indian War, the British General Edward Braddock came to America with two regiments of the British army. He also employed the help of the Virginia militia of which George Washington was a Colonel. General Braddock was seasoned in battle, but was unfamiliar with the Indian mode of warfare. Washington sought to warn General Braddock about the dangers of being ambushed and the need to have scouting parties. Prideful Braddock went into a rage and exclaimed, "What! An American buskin teach a British general how to fight!"[147] He continued, "These savages may indeed be a formidable enemy to your raw American militia, but upon the king's regular and disciplined troops, they do not stand a chance."[148] The proud sixty-year-old general was not about to take advice from a twenty-three-year-old soldier.

As the troops neared Fort Duquesne, Washington again approached the General and offered to take a team of scouts ahead to discover any awaiting ambushes. General Braddock again vehemently rejected the idea. General Braddock was so confident that his army would easily win the battle and take possession of Fort Duquesne that plans were made for a celebration with bonfires and fireworks.[149] The next day, disaster hit when they were ambushed. The General fought courageously but was wounded by a shot through the right arm and into his lung. Following the injury to General Braddock, Washington was able to form a rearguard, which allowed the army to evacuate and disengage. Washington carried General Braddock to a cart, which then carried him from the battle.

About a mile from the battle site, the military surgeon treated the General's wounds. Braddock was very weak as he lay on the cart during the return march. General Braddock called Washington to his side, took a decorative sash[150] from his uniform, and gave it to Washington.

Four days after the battle, on July 13, 1755, General Braddock died. The troops buried their courageous General in the middle of the road and held a funeral service to honor him. They then rolled over the fresh ground to keep his grave from being found and desecrated by any Indians that might pursue. Washington carried the sash with him throughout his life as a reminder to be a humble servant of the people.

From 1755 to 1758, Washington "served as the commander of the Virginia forces protecting the frontier from Indians."[151] From 1759 to 1775, Washington devoted his time almost exclusively to agriculture and the management of his rapidly expanding estate. Of course, he was reelected to the Virginia House of Burgesses repeatedly during these years, and he conscientiously attended the regular legislative sessions in the late fall and the early spring.[152]

On June 15, 1775, the Continental Congress met to elect a general for the Continental Army for the defense of American liberty. Each member of Congress cast their vote by ballot, and Washington was unanimously chosen to be the supreme commander of the forces to secure an independent and free nation. On June 16 in response to this request, Washington said, "Mr. President . . . I feel great distress . . . that my abilities and military experience may not be equal to the extensive and important trust. However, as the Congress desire it, I will enter upon the momentous duty, and exert every power I possess in their service, and for support of the glorious cause."[153] Washington wrote his brother saying, "It is my full intention to devote my life and fortune in the cause we are engaged in."[154]

In accepting the call, Washington refused to accept payment for his services. Congress was greatly impressed by his response and it reaffirmed that they had selected a man of great character, whose only desire was the welfare and happiness of his country.

Washington had the difficult task of turning thousands of farmers and shopkeepers into an army. Washington wrote that he had the "materials for a good army, a great number of men able-bodied, active, zealous in the cause, and of unquestionable courage."[155] However, Washington knew that it would take time to develop as an army saying, "We mend every day, and . . . in a little time we shall work up these raw materials into good stuff."[156] Brigadier General Nathanael Greene wrote of the reaction to Washington's early command, "His Excellency General Washington has arrived and is universally admired. The excellent character he bears, and the promising genius he possesses give great spirit to the troops."[157]

Washington knew he lacked the knowledge and experience needed so "he studied military texts from every source. He consulted with his most experienced officers, principally British-trained Horatio Gates and Charles Lee. He listened carefully, observed, meditated, adapted, revised, and studied some more. He moved ahead with what he had— raw, untrained, undisciplined troops—and lost battle after battle, almost lost his army, but learned from experience and tried again. . . . He found ingenious solutions to the immense, almost insurmountable, problems that faced him throughout the war."[158] Washington wrote of his study, "A knowledge of books is the basis upon which other knowledge is to be built."[159] "The inventory of Washington's books made at the time of his death by the appraisers of his estate shows that his library then numbered about nine hundred volumes."[160]

Washington was driven by "the cause." Washington continually referred to the army's mission with the phrases: the cause of liberty, the glorious cause, the goodness of the cause, the cause of freedom, the cause of his country, the cause of American freedom, the cause of America, the cause of mankind, and the cause of the patriots. When asked for advice by a young colonel, Washington wrote, "The best general advice I can give [is to] impress upon the mind of every man, from the first to the lowest, the importance of the cause and what it is they are contending for."[161]

Washington inspired greatness in others and instilled in them the great importance of the cause they were fighting for. A sergeant in the army recorded these events. "Our men . . . were without shoes or other comfortable clothing; and as traces of our march towards Princeton, the ground was literally marked with the blood of the soldiers' feet. . . . On the last day of December 1776 the time for which I and most of my regiment had enlisted expired, [Washington called the regiment into formation and urged them to reenlist. The drums beat and Washington called for volunteers willing to stay to step forward]. Not a man turned out. The soldiers worn down with fatigue and privations, had their hearts fixed on home and the comforts of the domestic circle, and it was hard to forego the anticipated pleasures of the society of our dearest friends. [Washington turned and began to ride away, and then stopped].

"The General wheeled his horse about, rode in front of the regiment and addressing us again said, 'My brave fellows, you have done all I asked you to do, and more than could be reasonably expected, but your country is at stake, your wives, your houses, and all that you hold dear. You have worn yourselves out with fatigues and hardships, but we know not how to spare you. If you will consent to stay one month longer, you will render that service to the cause of liberty, and to your country, which you can probably never do under any other circumstance. The present is emphatically the crisis, which is to decide our destiny.' The drums beat a second time. The soldiers felt the force of the appeal. One said to another, 'I will remain if you will.' Others remarked 'We cannot go home under such circumstances.' A few stepped forth, and their example was immediately followed by nearly all."[162]

When Washington began his command of the Continental Army, he knew they would experience extreme difficulties and sacrifice, but the challenges and suffering during the years of war exceeded even his worst expectations. The famous painter Charles Wilson Peale "walked among these ragged troops of Washington's who had made the escape across from New Jersey and wrote about it in his diary. He said he'd never seen such miserable human beings in all his life—starving, exhausted, and filthy. One man in particular he thought was just the most wretched human being he had ever laid eyes on. He described how the man's hair was all matted and how it hung down over his shoulders. The man was naked except for what they called a blanket coat. His feet were wrapped in rags, his face all covered with sores from sickness. Peale was studying him when, all of a sudden, he realized that the man was his own brother."[163]

Although the British Army greatly outnumbered the Continental Army and had superior supplies, weapons, training, and experience, the Continental Army had one distinct advantage—the cause. They were fighting for liberty and freedom. On July 2, 1776 Washington wrote his troops saying, "The fate of unborn millions will now depend, under

God, on the courage and conduct of this army. . . . Let us therefore rely upon the goodness of the cause, and the aid of the Supreme Being, in whose hands victory is. . . . Let us therefore animate and encourage each other and show the whole world that a freeman contending for LIBERTY on his own ground is superior to any slavish mercenary on earth."[164]

The Revolutionary War is one of the longest wars in American history, lasting eight and a half years. One percent of the population sacrificed their lives in the glorious cause of America. "If we were to fight for our independence today and the war was equally costly, there would be more than three million of us killed."[165]

The surviving soldiers welcomed with great pleasure the end of the war and the return to their homes. Washington wrote that he was "hastening with unspeakable delight to the still and placid walks of domestic life." His years of service were not only a sacrifice of time but of fortune. He wrote the Mount Vernon caretaker that "worse than going home to empty coffers . . . I shall be encumbered with debt."[166] In a letter to his nephew Fielding Lewis who had asked for a loan, Washington wrote, "You very much mistake my circumstances when you suppose me in a condition to advance money. I made no money from my estate during the nine years I was absent from it, and brought none home with me."[167]

Again, offers were made to pay Washington for his service, and even though Washington faced many financial pressures as a result of his time away from Mount Vernon, Washington would not accept payment for his service as commander-in-chief. Washington declared that "the greatest of earthly rewards [was] affection of a free people."[168]

The knowledge that he had done his duty "with the strictest rectitude and most scrupulous exactness"[169] to secure liberty for his nation and "unborn millions"[170] was "full compensation for all [his] toils and sufferings in the long and painful contest."[171]

Three days after Washington returned home, he wrote, "The scene is at last closed. I feel myself eased of a load of public care. I hope to spend the remainder of my days in cultivating the affections of good men, and in the practice of the domestic virtues."[172] However, the days without the load of public cares were few for General Washington.

In February 1787, Congress approved the holding of a convention "for the sole and express purpose of revising the Articles of Confederation."[173] Washington was in agreement that a constitution was needed to ensure the success of the nation. Many urged Washington to attend the convention, but he declined each of the invitations. One of the many requests came from Henry Knox who wrote to Washington, "It is conceived to be highly important to the success of the . . . convention. . . . The unbounded confidence the people have of your tried patriotism and wisdom would exceedingly facilitate . . . a convention of which you were a member."[174]

Washington began to see his participation in the Constitutional Convention was necessary to ensure the ongoing success and freedom of the nation. Washington wrote to Governor Randolph announcing he would participate at the convention as one of the delegates from Virginia. Henry Knox was very pleased to hear about Washington's change of mind and wrote, "Nothing but the critical situation of his country would have induced him. . . . It's happiness being in danger, he disregards all personal considerations."[175] *The Pennsylvania Herald* wrote of Washington, "This great patriot will never think his duty performed while anything remains to be done."

The Constitutional Convention began on May 25, 1787, and the first item of business was to select a presiding officer. Washington was nominated and unanimously selected. Since Washington had little experience in presiding over civil convocations, he began with an apology for any mistakes he might make. His role at the convention "was significant though quiet. Although he was viewed as a strong, determined leader, he . . . spoke only rarely before the convention or the committee of the whole."[176]

With the Constitution created and ratified, Washington planned to live out the reminder of his days as "an honest man on my own farm."[177] However, with the creation of the executive branch, a president was needed to lead the new government. Washington's name was quickly and often suggested as the man "best fitted"[178] to serve as the first president of the United States. Washington did not seek or want the office of president and wrote that if he accepted the office it "would be the greatest sacrifice of my personal feelings and wishes that ever I have been called upon to make."[179]

On April 6, 1789, Congress opened the elector's ballots and declared that George Washington was the unanimous choice for president. When Washington received notification of his selection, he replied in part, "I realize the arduous nature of the task which is imposed upon me, and feel my own inability to perform it. . . . All I can promise is only that which can be accomplished by an honest zeal."[180] Washington accepted the call to serve for the good of his country.

Congress voted to pay Washington a salary of $25,000 a year

(approximately $500,000 in today's dollars). Washington, however, chose to continue his work as an unpaid servant of the people. During his eight and a half years as commander-in-chief of the Continental Army, he took no pay. He would do the same as the first president of the United States.

George Washington said in his inaugural address of 1789, "When I was first honored with a call into the service of my country, then on the eve of an arduous struggle for its liberties, the light in which I contemplated my duty required that I should renounce . . . compensation. From this resolution I have in no instance departed. And being still under the impressions which produced it, I must decline [compensation]."[181]

"Time after time [Washington] gave up the comfortable security of his personal life in order to serve his country. On three separate occasions he retired from public life, fully expecting to live out his days in the quiet of his plantation. And on three separate occasions he answered the call to return the service of his country sacrificing his own desires for the peace and safety of America."[182]

Even though Washington became a national hero with fame, power, and great accomplishments, he remained a humble man. In response to the praise he received, he wrote, "I attribute all the glory to a Supreme Being. . . who was able by the humblest instruments. . . to establish and secure the liberty and happiness of these United States."[183]

After his eight years of service as the first president of the United States, he returned to his life as a farmer. His granddaughter Nelly Custis wrote of his return to the farm, "Grandpa is very well and much pleased with being once more Farmer Washington."[184] When a person came to the farm looking for General Washington, his grandson Parke Custis gave these directions, "You will meet, sir, with an old gentleman, riding alone, in plain drab clothes, a broad-brimmed white hat, a hickory switch in his hand, and carrying an umbrella with a long staff, which is attached to his saddlebow: that person, sir, is General Washington."[185]

Abigail Adams, wife of John Adams, wrote of Washington, "No man ever lived, more deservedly beloved and respected. . . . [He] maintained a modest diffidence of his own talents. . . . Possesst of power, possesst of an extensive influence, he never used it but for the benefit of his Country."[186]

Long live the memory of George Washington, the great servant leader!

ATTRIBUTE 15

INNOVATOR

"Do not go where the path may lead; go instead where there is no path and leave a trail."

-RALPH WALDO EMERSON

CHAPTER IX
BEING AN INNOVATOR

"Anything that is truly great or inspiring is
created in the mind of one individual laboring in
freedom."

-Albert Einstein

The great football coach Vince Lombardi taught, "Constantly seek ways to do better whatever needs to be done. If a person with this quality will continue positive application of this negative factor, that person will have a leadership role. The quality: dissatisfaction. To make the unsatisfactory satisfactory or better is the mark of leadership. Never be satisfied with less than top performance, and progress will be the reward." Each time we achieve a goal we should ask, How can it be done better? How can it be improved? "Never [be] satisfied with the status quo or with past attainments. Reaching a goal is merely a signal to set a higher one. Goal-setting is done in small increments so that people never become discouraged: at the same time, they are never permanently satisfied."[187]

Life is not like a staircase, where you can reach a certain step and then stop and maintain your position. Rather, life is like traveling upward on a downward escalator. If you're not stepping up, you will begin going down. Just as a tree is either growing or decaying, so we are either progressing or regressing. Coach John Wooden said, "If I am ever through learning, I am through. You either have to go forward or you'll go backward. You rarely move rapidly upward, but you can go downward very fast." In life, you cannot be at a standstill. We must continually seek improvement. We must continually find ways to innovate.

Philo "Phil" T. Farnsworth—Professional Mistake Maker

"The difficult we do right away; the impossible takes slightly longer. . . . We never know what our capabilities really are until faced with an emergency."

-Philo T. Farnsworth

Phil was born on August 19, 1906, in a small log home built by his father in Beaver, Utah. From an early age, Phil was curious about how things worked, and he asked a lot of questions about man-made devices such as electric streetlights, the automobile, and the telephone. He learned who the inventors of these items were and studied their works. In learning about Alexander Graham Bell and Thomas Edison, "he came to the conclusion that inventors were truly special people, and he hoped that someday he could be an inventor."[188] Phil also intently studied the works of Albert Einstein and was so impressed by his theories that he committed them to memory.[189]

The family moved to a white home on a farm in Rigby, Idaho in 1918. The attic of the home became Phil's bedroom. In his room, he was very excited to find stacks of science journals and technical magazines that had been left by the previous owner. "To Phil, these magazines were a gift from above. . . . The only problem was that he had very little time to read them. He had chores and school and other responsibilities as the oldest of five. So he set his alarm each night, usually for 4 a.m., giving him an hour or more to read and think before he had to begin his routine. Trying not to wake anyone, he would rise from his bed, switch on the light, get back under the covers, open a magazine, and allow the stories of inventions and scientists to fire his imagination. During the day, he sought ways to apply his rapidly growing knowledge."[190]

The Rigby home and farm were powered by a generator. One of Phil's favorite activities was to watch the repairmen work when the generator had broken down, which seemed to happen all too often. He asked numerous questions and intently watched the repairman. He learned all he could about how the generator worked from the repairmen and his reading.

One day, the generator stopped working shortly after a visit from the repairman. The family didn't have the money to pay for the repairman to return, and they didn't have the money to replace it. Phil's father and uncle were discussing what they should do, when Phil, then age twelve, asked if he could try and fix it. His older cousins that were present laughed at Phil, but his father suggested it wouldn't hurt to give him a chance. His uncle reluctantly agreed, and Phil went to work. The family watched as Phil worked on the generator, and by the time he had finished, his entire family had gathered to watch. "Everyone was watching intently as Phil stood up and confidently pressed the 'on' button. The generator sprang into action and started humming more smoothly than ever. Everyone but Phil was surprised. Uncle Albert thumped Phil on the shoulder and appointed him engineer-in-chief of the farm. His father gave him a hug and said, 'Good work, son.'"[191]

Phil continued to learn all he could and used the money he earned to buy books and magazines on science and inventions. Phil set up an elaborate laboratory by salvaging old machinery, tools, and supplies. He used his laboratory to test ideas, conduct experiments, and work on inventions. One of his successful inventions was to convert the family's hand-powered washing machine to an electric-powered one by attaching a motor. His sister was most grateful for the invention as it saved her many hours of pushing and pulling the handle.

In his reading, Phil discovered several articles about the transmission of pictures in addition to sound over the airwaves. He read about the work that had been done in the previous decades but that nothing of significance had been produced. Phil saw this as a fantastic opportunity and started to arise at 2 a.m. each morning to study and ponder to see if he could discover a way of transmitting pictures.

On a summer morning in 1921, Phil went about his daily routine. He arose early to read literature on transmitting pictures and then went to work on the farm. The work for the day included the harrowing of a potato field. As he went back and forth over the field, he was reviewing the ideas he was currently working on and was brainstorming ideas for an alternative approach that might be more successful.

"As Phil turned the horses to cultivate another row parallel to the previous one, he gazed back at what he had already done. He saw row after row of furrows. An inspiration struck him like a jolt of electricity to the heart. It hit with so much force that he froze and nearly fell off his seat. . . . He saw televisions in that field. Just as a field needed to be plowed line by line, light had to be captured line by line. Phil knew that light energy could be converted into electrical current. What if patterns of electrons could represent patterns of light? After an image was scanned, the process could be reversed. The electron beams could be shot through a tube and converted back into an image that could be re-created on a screen in evenly painted lines. Electrons moved so fast that an entire image could manifest itself this way in a wink."[192]

He was excited to share the idea with someone and tried to explain the idea to his father, but his father did not have the technical knowledge to understand what he was describing. His father did counsel him to keep the idea a secret, which Phil felt was a good idea as his idea could be taken by the many who were working on this same problem.

In the fall, Phil began as a freshman at Rigby High School. Phil was interested in taking the senior chemistry class so he approached the teacher, Justin Tolman, and asked if he could take his class. His request was denied. Phil then approached the principal and expressed his interest in the class but was told he could not skip ahead.

In an attempt to complete the prerequisites quickly, he persuaded his introductory science teacher to give him all the coursework for the class at once. He aced all of the assignments and tests. Phil's work impressed his teacher greatly, so she approached the principle to request that Phil be allowed to take the senior class and again the petition was refused. Phil was determined to take the class as he felt he needed the knowledge for the work he was doing on television. Phil approached Justin Tolman again and asked if he could just sit in on his class. Tolman agreed and figured he would quickly bore with the subject and stop attending. After a few classes, it was clear to Tolman that Phil knew more than any of the seniors in the class.

Tolman approached the principal and requested that Phil be allowed to take his class and committed to personally tutoring him after school. The principal finally agreed. Phil came early to school and stayed late every day to work with Tolman. Tolman would give Phil assignments and reading materials, and Phil was constantly bringing questions. Tolman said of his time with Phil, "He would devour what was in these books and come back for more."[193]

Phil grew to trust Tolman, and he wanted to get his opinion on his new invention. He had not shared his idea with anyone except his father. One day after school, Phil found an empty study room and began drawing the details of his invention on the chalkboard. The diagrams and formulas nearly filled the entire board. As he was completing his drawing, Tolman came into the room and took a seat and watched as he finished. When Phil had finished, he looked at Tolman and said with excitement, "This is my new invention." Tolman asked what this had to do with his chemistry assignments, and Phil responded that it had nothing to do with an assignment but was his idea for television.

Phil explained in detail how his invention would work and how it would transmit images into people's homes just as radio had done with sound. At the conclusion of his presentation, he asked what Tolman thought. "It just might work," Tolman answered. Phil drew a simplified version of the chalkboard sketch and gave it to Tolman. Tolman saved this sketch and was able to present it years later in court to prove that Phil was indeed the first to develop the idea of electronic television when Phil's patents were disputed and infringed on by RCA and others.

In the fall of 1922, Phil's father sold the ranch in Rigby and moved the family back to Utah. In the winter of 1924, Phil's father caught pneumonia while driving a wagon during a blizzard and passed away. The family was greatly saddened. Phil's mother spent three months in bed with depression. With his father gone, money was tight, but Phil was determined to go to college. He enrolled at Brigham Young University (BYU) in Provo, Utah. He was able to pay for his tuition for his first year of college through a job as a janitor and student loans.

While at BYU, he concentrated on gleaning all possible information from his professors. When he told them about his ideas of broadcasting not just sound but sound and pictures, they were very skeptical and told him he was over his head, but they still did their best to answer his incessant questions. When asked if the skepticism of his university professors discouraged him, Phil answered, "I was more disappointed than anything. I had hoped to find in them someone who could understand what I was talking about. Their disbelief made me only more determined to show them I could do what I said I could."[194]

While in school, money was very tight. At times he didn't even have enough money for food, and he was losing weight. In the spring of 1926, the nineteen-year-old Farnsworth decided he could no longer afford to stay at the University and took a full-time job in Salt Lake City with a charity called Community Chest.

While this job had nothing to do with electronics or television, it resulted in him finding his first investors. At the end of a long day at work, Phil and the two men who ran the Community Chest, George Everson and Leslie Gorrell, were sitting around a table and having a friendly conversation. Everson and Gorrell were well connected, having worked on numerous fundraising efforts for the Community Chest. Everson asked Phil if he planned to go back to school, and Phil answered that he did not because he could not afford it. Phil then went on to tell them that what he really wanted to do was develop his invention, but he was finding it very difficult to find financing for the project. Gorrell then asked him about his invention. Phil told the group about his idea for television, and when he was finished, he urged them to keep his idea a secret even though he had not explained the technical aspect of the invention.

Over the next few days, Gorrell thought about the ideas Phil shared. Gorrell had a background in engineering, and the more he thought about the invention of television, the more intrigued he became. He decided he needed to learn more. Gorrell approached Everson and suggested they again meet with Phil to discuss his invention, and they set a time to take him to dinner. Everson described the meeting saying, "As the discussion started, Farnworth's personality seemed to change. His eyes . . . began burning with eagerness and conviction; his speech which was halting, became fluent to the point of eloquence as he described [the idea] that had occupied his mind for the last four years. . . . He became a super salesman, inspiring his listeners with an ever-increasing interest in what he was saying. . . . [It was] one of the most interesting evenings I ever spent."[195]

Everson asked Phil, "Isn't it likely that General Electric or Bell Laboratories have accomplished all you propose, and probably have it nearly ready for use?"[196] Phil answered with a detailed description of the work that had been done and was being done on television and then answered, "They are all barking up the wrong tree. All these men are trying to transmit pictures by mechanical means. This will never do. The speeds required for scanning an image to produce a good picture are so great that there must be no moving parts."[197] Phil went on to explain how his system solved this problem by an entirely electrical system that would manipulate electrons within vacuum tubes.

Phil expressed his fear that someone would take his idea and that he desired to obtain a patent but did not have the money to produce the working model needed to apply. Everson asked, "Just how much do you think it would take to prove out your system?"

"It's pretty hard to say," Phil replied, "but I should think five thousand dollars would be enough."

Five thousand dollars was a lot of money (approximately $65,000 in today's dollars); however, Everson liked the idea and liked Phil so decided to fund the initial prototype. Everson wrote, "I was willing to take a chance and gamble . . . on the apparent genius, integrity, intelligence, and industry of the boy. . . . I [had] about six thousand dollars in a special account [I'd] accumulated with the idea that I'd take a long-shot chance on something, hoping to make a killing. This [was] about as wild a gamble as I can imagine."[198]

Later in the week, Everson, Farnsworth, and Gorrell sat down to finalize an agreement. Farnsworth was to receive $150 a month ($2,000 a month in today's dollars), so he could give his whole time to the development of his idea. Farnsworth was to be a 50 percent owner, with Everson and Gorrell each owing 25 percent of the partnership. Gorrell drafted the initial contract, which was later reviewed by an attorney. As they discussed the practical aspects of the partnership agreement, Farnsworth told his partners he would like to move to Southern California, so he could have access to the California Institute of Technology, which had a fantastic library and was the center of innovation for the motion picture industry.

The arrangements for Farnsworth to work full time on the project were underway, and he was soon to leave for Los Angeles when "a new complication arose. Farnsworth disclosed that before he left Salt Lake City he wanted to get married."[199] Phil was determined to take Pem with him to California.

Phil and Pem were engaged on Pem's birthday, February 25, but had agreed that they would continue their education at least another year before taking the profound step of marriage, as Phil was only nineteen and Pem eighteen. It was three months later, on May 24, when Pem received a call from Phil saying, "Pem, darling, can you be ready to be married in three days?"

Recovering from the shock, Pem responded, "Phil Farnsworth, you've got to be kidding! Of course I can't be married in three days or three weeks for that matter! Who would take care of my family?"

Phil cut her short with, "Not another word. I'll take care of everything. Call your father and tell him I must see him in Provo tomorrow evening. Don't worry; I'm not crazy. See you tomorrow at six!" Phil hung up the phone, and Pem was left in a daze, but as she thought on the call she was filled with excitement and thought that perhaps he had obtained funding for his television invention. She did not think it possible to leave her family as her mother had died just four months earlier.

The next evening, Phil met with his mother, Pem, and Pem's father. Phil asked that they hear the whole story before making a decision. Phil shared with them the partnership he had entered in with Everson and Gorrell and their desire for him to be in Los Angeles by the weekend and how important it was for Pem to go with him. Pem wrote of the evening, "I had been sitting on the edge of my seat, barely able to contain my excitement through all this narrative. . . . My excitement was spilling all over the place. . . . Our parents sat in momentarily stunned silence, no doubt trying to sort out the good news from the shock of our marrying so young and worse yet, of our going all the way to California."[200]

Phil asked Pem's father for his blessing on the wedding and move to California. He answered, "You bet . . . I wouldn't stand in your way. This is your big chance, and I know what it means to both of you. The little girls can help me keep house."

Pem wrote that as her father gave his blessing, "A sense of ecstasy enveloped me. Could this really be happening? . . . My heart sang a blissful rhapsody, and I jumped up to give Daddy a big hug and kiss."[201]

Phil then turned to his mother stating, "Mother, I know how hard it's been for you since Papa died, and I've not forgotten the charge he gave me to take care of you and the family. I'll be able to help you somewhat, from the beginning, and hopefully within a year or two can make you financially independent. I will also be able to help Pem's family. What do you say?"

His mother replied, "I'm sure that if your father were here he'd say, 'Go with my blessings,' and that's what I say." Phil and Pem were married on May 27, 1926 at his mother's home in Provo. Following the wedding and reception, they drove to Salt Lake City and checked into a hotel and Pem shared the following, "Releasing me from a tight embrace, he held me off, and looking deep into my eyes, he said, 'Pemmie, I have to tell you there is another woman in my life.' Then before I could faint from the shock, he added, 'and her name is Television.'"[202]

On the morning of May 28, they boarded a train to Los Angeles to begin their new life together. They secured a furnished apartment in Hollywood with a garage. The apartment would function as their home and as the laboratory. Phil set up his research area in the dining room and established a motor generator in the garage. Equipment and supplies filled the apartment. The number of supplies brought into the apartment and the disturbance from the generator led some of the neighbors to be suspicious of what was going on in the apartment. One day, both the front and back door bells rang at the same time. Phil went to the front door and Pem went to the back door. To their surprise, each faced a burly policeman. The policemen stated they wanted to search the apartment because a neighbor reported a still was probably being operated on the premises. This was during prohibition so the neighbor had thought the most logical explanation for all the activity was the making of alcohol. The police did not find any alcohol but were still concerned that something illegal might be going on and asked about all the equipment and apparatuses. Phil explained that he was working on a television system, which seemed to satisfy the policemen.[203]

Farnsworth worked diligently, and by the end of the summer, he had finished the first complete electronic television system, "including a camera, transmitter, and a smaller reception tube that would accept the signal. If it would only project but a single ray of light, Farnsworth would be overjoyed beyond belief. He invited Everson and Gorrell over to the apartment to witness the results of an entire summer's work. When everyone was assembled, and everything was connected, Farnsworth switched on the electrical generator.

"First everyone heard a loud bang. That was followed by a few pops, then a slow hissing and a sizzle. Pungent smoke rose from the assortment of devices. By the time Farnsworth could shut the power off, it was too late. He had blown up the entire contraption, including his prized Image Dissector. Farnsworth . . . was hugely disappointed and . . . he dreaded the reaction from his two investors. Pointing to the pile of smoky junk, he said, 'That's all I have to show you for your investment.'

"As Everson looked over the mess, Gorrell deflected his attention away from it. 'It's not the end of the world,' he said. We still have Phil's ideas. Let's sit down and decide what we can do about it.' The partners cleared away the remains . . . then they sat down at the table to assess their situation."[204]

With the remaining money, they decided to focus on getting as much patent protection as possible for Phil's ideas. It was determined that Farnsworth was to write up a complete description of his proposed television system with schematic drawings to accompany it. They found a patent attorney in the area and set up a meeting. The attorney said he would also invite an expert from Cal Tech to evaluate the merits of the idea.

The meeting with the attorney and experts concluded that the ideas were scientifically sound and that the ideas were original, although a patent search was to be done to confirm this. This provided the partners with some reassurance, and over the following week, much time was given to the discussion of ways and means of getting additional financing. It was finally agreed that an effort should be made to secure $25,000 in additional funding, and Everson was given the task of securing the money.

Everson began visiting with his contacts to request funding for the highly speculative adventure. Everson was met with rejection after rejection. He had raised a lot of money for charity but soon realized it was going to be much more difficult to raise the needed money to develop Farnsworth's invention. Everson wrote of the experience, "All were fascinated by the possibility of the new art, but they were afraid that I had been led astray by a fantastic scheme that had hardly one chance in a million of success."[205]

Everson decided to visit a banker friend in San Francisco to see if he could find some investors with deep pockets. Everson presented the fantastic story of Farnsworth's developments and then waited. The banker brought his hands together and began tapping his fingers as he looked at Everson over the rims of his glasses and said, "Well, that is a damn fool idea, but somebody ought to put money into it, someone who can afford to lose it."[206]

The banker had Everson meet with an engineer who they used to evaluate various ideas presented to the bank. The engineer was impressed with Farnsworth's memorandum detailing the project and was interested in meeting with Farnsworth as soon as possible. Everson arranged for Farnsworth to drive to San Francisco, and the banker arranged a lunch meeting for Farnsworth and Everson to meet with an investor by the name of Roy Bishop, along with the engineer. After several hours of discussion, Mr. Bishop stated, "I am convinced that the idea is sound, but doubt your ability to work it out commercially."

Farnsworth rose from his seat, walked over to the desk, picked up his briefcase, and with a courteous gesture, thanked Mr. Bishop for his kindness in spending so much time discussing the matter. He expressed regret that Bishop could not see the possibilities that others saw in the invention.

As Farnsworth and Everson were about to close the door behind them, Bishop said, "Wait a minute." Bishop then stated that he would like to have an engineer by the name of Harlan Honn look into the matter and said, "If you can convince him that your proposition is sound and can be worked out, I think we will find ways of backing you."

Within thirty minutes, Farnsworth, Honn, and Everson were in earnest discussions of the television plans. Honn promptly grasped the significance of Farnsworth's ideas. After he had read the specifications and had his questions answered, he said, "Why, sure this system will work. I think very well of it." Everson presented his findings to Bishop, and Bishop requested that Farnsworth and Everson meet with him and his partners in the director's room at the bank the following afternoon. Farnsworth began by saying that he proposed to do for vision what radio was doing so successfully for sound, presented his plan to bring this about, and successfully answered their many questions.

As their discussion neared conclusion, Bishop asked, "How much do you think it will take to produce a recognizable television picture?" Farnsworth answered that he believed he could produce a television picture in one year with $1,000 a month, but asked for $25,000 (approximately $325,000 in today's dollars) to ensure they had enough funding for unseen problems or expenses that were sure to arise. The investors said they didn't think it was enough, but agreed to give $25,000 for 60 percent ownership and the expectation of a television transmission within a year. The remaining 40 percent ownership was divided so Farnsworth owned 20 percent, Gorrell 10 percent, and Everson 10 percent. It was arranged that Farnsworth would be given an allowance of $1,000 a month for the laboratory, out of which he was to receive a salary of $200 a month (approximately $2,600 in today's dollars) and work at a 600-square foot office the investors had available in San Francisco. Farnsworth returned to Los Angeles, arranged for the shipment of his lab equipment, loaded up his personal belongings, and drove with his wife to San Francisco.[207]

It was now the fall of 1926, and Farnsworth began working at an intense pace. The lab journals show that he worked twelve hours a day, six days a week. Farnsworth did not work on Sundays to observe the Sabbath Day. Farnsworth created a year plan with a systematic process to create, test, and perfect each of the components needed, with a final test for the entire system working together. The journals showed how he tried one technique after another, documenting what was learned from each attempt and failure. Farnsworth described his work in the lab to his wife, Pem, on one occasion saying, "I'm a professional mistake maker."

Farnsworth put in many, many hours of physical labor, but he also recognized the importance of thinking and seeking inspiration from God. When he had a problem that left him stumped, he would ponder on the problem before going to bed and then set his alarm for an hour before normal rising time to spend the extra hour in quiet thinking. "Usually this would bring the solution of the problem that had occupied his attention and baffled him the previous day."[208] Farnsworth recognized the hand of God in his work saying, "I know that God exists. I know that I have never invented anything. I have been a medium by which these things were given to the culture as fast as the culture could earn them. I give all the credit to God."[209] Farnsworth believed "we all have God-given talents, which we are duty bound to develop for the good of all people."[210]

Farnsworth was making progress each day; however, Farnsworth and his investors were worried that someone would file for a similar patent before they did. Farnsworth traveled back to Los Angeles to complete the formal patent application with the law office he had previous meetings with. He returned to San Francisco with the complete patent application, which he signed before a notary and put in the mail. The official filing date was January 7, 1927. This was Farnsworth's first patent application at the age of twenty years old.

"By August [1927] . . . all the pieces [were] in place, and their energy level and sense of anticipation were rising every day. There were only two months to go before the original one-year deadline, a target date that loomed large in the minds of Farnsworth's investors."[211] Farnsworth and his staff began testing the components and hooking pieces together for the first time. After another month of intense work, they were ready for the first test of the entire television system. This test occurred on September 7th.

"They had partitioned the room into two parts. Cliff placed a slide with the image of a triangle in front of the Image Dissector in one section of the lab while everyone else gathered around the receiving tube behind the partition. The two tubes were connected by an amplifier and wires."[212]

As Cliff put the triangle slide in, the receiving screen "was disturbed and settled down with a messy blur in the center. By no stretch of the imagination could it be recognized as the black triangle that we were supposed to see. . . . Phil suggested some adjustments on the amplifier and the scanning generator circuits. There was a lot of feverish puttering around with no improvements in the results. . . . After a couple of hours of struggle, [Farnsworth believed he had corrected the problems and called everyone into the receiving room for another test.] Cliff put the slide in again. A fuzzy, blurry, but wholly recognizable image of the black triangle instantly filled the center of the picture field."[213]

Farnsworth shouted with excitement, "That's it folks! We've done it. There you have electronic television." Cliff ran into the receiving room and on seeing the picture said, "Well, I'll be damned." One of the staff was in shock saying, "If I wasn't seeing it with my own two eyes, I wouldn't believe it." Pem gave her husband a giant hug and jumped around the room in jubilation. Farnsworth had turned twenty-one two weeks earlier, and now there was visual proof that his ideas for television, first created when he was fourteen years old, did indeed work.

Farnsworth wanted to improve the picture before providing a demonstration to his investors. Farnsworth and his staff continued to work to improve the system. The lab journals of 1928 illustrate how Farnsworth worked to solve problem after problem to improve the television system. During the year, he received several messages from his investors asking when they were going to see some money from the invention. By August 1928, Farnsworth was ready to provide a demonstration for the investors and called a meeting. Farnsworth wrote that all of the adjustments had improved the picture tenfold.

As the group of investors stood around the receiving tube, Farnsworth said, "Here's something a banker will understand." On the screen appeared an image of a dollar sign. The group erupted into laughter and began slapping their knees with excitement. The demonstration was a success, and the banker requested that Farnsworth arrange for a demonstration for the press and the public in hopes of finding a buyer. "Farnsworth was not interested in selling his patents— he wanted to license them and collect royalties that would support his future work. . . . He was determined to maintain his independence."[214]

The partnership between Farnsworth and his investors was officially incorporated as Television Laboratories, and stock was issued to each of the partners. They did not have a desire to take the company public, but the investors were free to sell the stock as they wished. One of the investors sold a small portion of his holding for $5,000 ($65,000 in today's dollars), which indicated a valuation for the company at $500,000 ($6.5 million in today's dollars) and soon the company was valued at $1 million ($13 million in today's dollars).

"With the price of shares in Television Laboratories valued so highly, Farnsworth decided to sell off some of his stock. He initially sold less than 5 percent of his holdings, but the money went far. He bought a boxy black Chrysler roadster, which he promptly drove to the factory were Pem was working. He took her hand and led her out to the shiny new car. He told her that she could quit her job now, and she gladly did. Soon after, they went looking for a home to buy and found a newly developed set of . . . houses . . . not far from the water. Phil signed over some shares to the developer as a down payment. He also gave shares to his siblings, Pem's siblings, Pem's father, and his own mother back in Utah, making her financially independent the rest of her life."[215] Pem wrote of their financial success, "Being able to share with our families made our own good fortune mean even more to us."

Phil continued to make many improvements to television and develop the technology, so it could be accessible to the masses. Farnsworth had to continually fight off his investors' desire to sell his patents to a large corporation and take the large immediate return. Farnsworth did not want to lose control of his invention. His desire was to sell non-exclusive licenses to companies for the right to use his inventions in their products. For Farnsworth television was just the beginning; the royalties from television could be used to fund the development of additional inventions to make the world a better place.

After many years of long, hard work, and many struggles, Farnsworth was able to license his patents to organizations all across the world, including AT&T and RCA, earning millions in royalties. However, Farnsworth was not interested in building a massive personal fortune. His concerns were providing for his family, providing for those who worked with him, and financing future inventions. For example, a doctor in Texas asked Phil if he could develop a device that could be put down the mouth and esophagus to view the inside of the stomach. Phil agreed to construct one for him. The doctor came to Phil's lab when it was completed and was very pleased with the results. He offered to "pay Phil anything he wanted. Phil told him it was pay enough to know he was helping some poor, suffering person."[216] "The wealth that motivated Philo T. Farnsworth was not the wealth of capital gains but the wealth of ideas of knowledge."[217]

After he finished his work on television, Farnsworth continued his work as an innovator. He developed the first baby incubator, the electron microscope, radar technology, infrared night light technology, peacetime uses for atomic energy, gastroscope technology, astronomical telescope technology, and fusion reaction tubes called fusors.[218] Phil's health declined rapidly toward the end of his life. Calculating that he had three to five years left to live, Phil told his wife, Pem, he wanted to give the world four more things. He wanted to finish fusion, which would supply inexpensive, safe, and almost unlimited power. He wanted to remove the unfiltered viruses from culinary water, solve the ever-increasing problem of human waste, and build a combination lab and university where students would learn by working to create useful products.

Farnsworth would not live long enough to complete his final gifts to the world. In January 1971, Phil became very ill with pneumonia and died on March 11 at the young age of sixty-four. His wife wrote of an experience shortly after his death: "In Phil's study, I noticed the small plaque he always had on his desk, which read, 'Men and trees die—ideas live on for the ages.' 'Oh, Phil, how true,' I thought, but he had taken so many unfulfilled ideas with him to his grave."[219]

Are you the next great innovator who is to continue and complete the work of Phil Farnsworth? "Starting . . . with an empty loft, a year, and twenty-five thousand dollars, Phil had created an entire industry."[220] By the end of his life, he held three hundred patents[221] for his various inventions. Phil Farnsworth should inspire each of us to ask, "What is going to be my next innovation?"

ATTRIBUTE 16
MISSION DRIVEN

"He who has a why to live for can
bear almost any how."

-Friedrich Nietzsche

CHAPTER X
FINDING AND FULFILLING YOUR MISSION

"God gives us an intrinsic desire to contribute,
add value, and connect with others in some
meaningful endeavor. Finding meaning and
purpose in our work is the key to both personal
fulfillment and professional success."

-Larry Julian

There are specific ways in which each of us is to contribute to society. "Everyone has his own specific vocation or mission in life to carry out a concrete assignment which demands fulfillment. Therein he cannot be replaced, nor can his life be repeated. Thus, everyone's task is as unique as is his specific opportunity to implement it."[222]

"Most of us would like to make a positive impact on the lives of others and on our world. If we do not feel that this is in some way happening, we tend to experience a sense of emptiness, low self-worth, futility, and sometimes even depression."[223] Every life has a purpose and a mission.

"We detect rather than invent our missions in life.... I think each of us has an internal monitor or sense, a conscience that gives us an awareness of our uniqueness and the singular contributions that we can make.... Writing... a mission statement changes you because it forces you to think through your priorities deeply, carefully, and to align your behavior with your beliefs. As you do, other people begin to sense that you're not being driven by everything that happens to you. You have a sense of mission about what you're trying to do, and you are excited about it."[224]

"I believe it is well within the natural order of things to have everybody humming while they work. As a noted economist recently stated, 'Unemployment is a characteristic unique to the human species only. All the other creatures and creations seem to know what they are supposed to be doing.'"[225]

Roles/Stewardships

"Preachers are put here to minister to our souls; doctors to heal our diseases; teachers to open up our minds; and so on. Everybody has their role to play."
–Sam Walton, founder of Walmart

We each have various roles/stewardships and responsibilities. I, for example, am the president of multiple organizations, an author, a teacher, a minister, a husband, and a father. Within each of these stewardships, I have a mission and specific goals related to each. Identifying your mission and goals in each stewardship will help you maintain a balance and will help you focus on the most important things.

For Columbus, one of his missions was to discover new lands. For George Washington, one of his missions was to create a free nation. For Phil Farnsworth, one of his missions was to develop television. Walt Disney's mission statement for Disneyland was "to make people happy."

The co-founder of Microsoft, Paul Allen, discovered his mission while in high school. He spent many hours in the computer lab and found that he had a great love for programming. He wrote, "Crafting my own computer code felt more creative than anything I'd tried before. . . . Soon I was spending every lunchtime and free period around the Teletype. . . . I had discovered my calling. I was a programmer."[226]

As Sam Walton, the founder of Walmart, neared the end of his life dying of cancer, he reflected on his life's work and wondered if he should have spent his time on something else to improve the world. He wondered if he made the right choice to invest so much time in building Walmart. After much thought, he concluded that his work at Walmart was a part of his ministry—that through his retail business, he was able to improve and bless the lives of many others. His mission statement for Walmart was to provide a better shopping experience for everyday people living in small towns and to improve their standard of living by providing quality goods at low prices in a pleasant shopping environment.[227]

CAMERON C. TAYLOR

Christopher Columbus—A Man with a Mission and a Love of the Sea

"One doesn't discover new lands without consenting
to lose sight, for a very long time, of the shore."

–André Gide

Columbus was born in 1451 in the ancient city of Genoa in northwestern Italy. In his youth, Columbus was drawn to and loved the sea. History is clear that Columbus had very little, if any, formal schooling; however, he was an avid reader. His library and love of reading were continued by his son Ferdinand, who "accumulated a large and splendid library which numbered over 15,000 volumes at the time of his death in 1539, and which eventually went to the cathedral chapter of Seville."[228] Christopher Columbus wrote hundreds of notes throughout the books that have survived. Columbus also learned the art of seamanship in the school of experience joining various fleets and voyages. Columbus's studies and time at sea filled him with a drive to discover new lands by sea.

Columbus saw that many were seeking to establish new trade routes from Europe to India and China. The land routes used for many years had become difficult and dangerous, as areas along the route had fallen under the control of the Ottoman Empire. Europe traded valuable goods such as silk, spices, and opiates with India and China, so the reestablishment of an effective trade route was greatly desired.

Columbus studied all the resources available for options on a new trade route. Many countries and navigators were seeking to reach India by sailing around Africa without success. In 1474, at age twenty-three, Columbus developed a plan to reach the east by sailing west. Columbus was confident that Asia (or the Indies, as the Europeans called it) could be reached faster and easier by sailing west.

Columbus diligently sought support for his enterprise but was met with rejection after rejection. "The first definite offer known to us is the one that he made to D. Joao II, King of Portugal."229 The king submitted Columbus's proposal to his Maritime Advisory Committee, which was organized to oversee matters of discovery and navigation. Columbus's proposal was rejected, "yet Columbus had made an impression on the king. They parted friends, and very likely D. Joao encouraged him to call again,"230 in case the attempted voyages to reach Asia by sailing around Africa failed.

After meeting with Columbus, the king secretly commissioned a ship to sail west to see if such a voyage might be possible. Columbus's son Ferdinand wrote of this voyage, "Because the people [the King] sent lacked the knowledge, steadfastness, and ability of the Admiral, they wandered about on the sea for many days and returned to the Cape Verdes and thence to Lisbon, making fun of the enterprise and declaring no land could be found in those waters."231

In 1479 at the age of twenty-eight, Columbus married Filipa Moniz Perestrelo, and in 1480 their son, Diego Columbus, was born. In 1484, Columbus's wife of five years died at only twenty-nine years old. "It must have been with heavy heart that early in 1485 Columbus left Portugal for Spain, where he hoped for better fortune. The . . . years were filled with expectation and disappointment as he tried to win the support of the Spanish monarchs, Fernando and Isabella, for his endeavor. It took almost a year before Columbus obtained his first audience, and then the king and queen, preoccupied with the war against the Moors in Granada, simply referred his petition to an ad hoc commission of scholars [who had his proposal under advisement for years]."[232]

"Early in 1488 [Columbus] wrote to D. Joao II expressing a desire to renew his application and to visit Lisbon. . . . The king replied in the most cordial terms, addressing Columbus as 'our particular friend,' lauding his 'industry and good talent,' urging . . . him to come immediately."[233]

It would seem that the king's interest in Columbus's west sailing voyage was renewed as he had no news from the Bartholomew Dias fleet that had left in the summer of 1487 to search for a route to India by sailing around Africa. Columbus did not go to Portugal immediately but did arrive by December 1488. Columbus arrived in Lisbon just in time to witness the return of the Dias fleet to report on their success. "Now that Africa had been circumnavigated and the eastern sea route to India was open, the king of Portugal had no more use for Columbus, who returned to Spain."[234]

Columbus had now been seeking support for his enterprise for fifteen years, "but Columbus would not be put off. He continued to promote his project . . . tenaciously."[235] It was his sense of mission that kept him going. You cannot fully understand Columbus's drive and commitment without understanding his strong faith in God. A twentieth-century biographer of Columbus wrote, "There can be no doubt that the faith of Columbus was genuine and sincere, and that his frequent communion with forces unseen was a vital element in his achievement. It gave him confidence in his destiny, assurance that his performance would be equal to the promise of his name. This conviction that God destined him to be an instrument for spreading the faith was far more potent than the desire to win glory, wealth, and worldly honors."[236]

Columbus wrote, "The Lord opened to my understanding (I could sense his hand upon me), so that it became clear to me that it was feasible to navigate from here to the Indies, and he unlocked within me the determination to execute this idea. . . . Who doubts that this illumination was from the Holy Spirit? I attest that [the Spirit], with marvelous rays of light, consoled me through the holy and sacred Scriptures . . . encouraging me to proceed, and continually, without ceasing for a moment, they inflame me with a sense of great urgency. . . . No one should be afraid to take on any enterprise in the name of our Savior."[237]

"Columbus . . . was back in Spain in early 1489 waiting, hoping, and praying for a favorable report from the . . . committee [commissioned by Queen Isabella] and for a swift conclusion of the last campaign against Granada."[238] The report from the committee would not come for two more years, late in the year 1490. "The committee 'judged his promises and offers were impossible and vain and worthy of rejection,' says Las Casas, and advised the Sovereigns 'that it was not a proper object for the royal authority to favor an affair that rested on such weak foundations and which appeared uncertain and impossible to any educated person.'"[239] Columbus wrote of his struggle to find supporters, "Those who heard of my [adventurous enterprise] called it foolish, mocked me, and laughed."[240]

The committee gave many reasons to reject the proposal, including the following: "A voyage to Asia would require three years. The Western

Ocean is infinite and perhaps unnavigable. If he reached . . . the land on the other side of the globe from Europe he could not get back. . . . So many centuries after the creation, it was unlikely that anyone could find hitherto unknown lands of any value.

"Ferdinand and Isabella neither accepted nor rejected the . . . report. They caused Columbus to be informed . . . that his enterprise might again be brought to their attention at a more propitious moment, when the war with Granada was over. . . . Columbus waited another six to nine months [and] by the end of that time he swore . . . he would wait no longer on the Queen's pleasure. . . . Columbus determined to go to France and offer his Enterprise to Charles VIII. . . . Fray Juan Perez, head of the friary, deplored Columbus's intention to quit Spain forever. Fray Juan, who many years before had been confessor or comptroller to the Queen (perhaps both), promised to obtain for Columbus another royal audience if he would stay. . . . Before long the Queen wrote directly to Columbus . . . The Queen included in her letter the sum of 20,000 maravedis in order that Columbus might procure some decent clothing and a mule"[241] to ease Columbus's poverty.

In the later part of 1491, Columbus arrived in his new clothes to appear before the Queen. The Queen sent his proposal to a new committee. At the beginning of 1492, Columbus "was informed that his Enterprise was absolutely and definitely rejected. The Sovereigns themselves confirmed this at an audience which they meant to be final. . . . That was the result of six and a half years' watching and waiting in Spain. Columbus saddled his mule, packed up the saddlebags . . . and set forth on the road to Cordova. . . .

"Columbus had made another friend at court, Luis de Santangel. The very day that Columbus departed . . . Santangel went to find the Queen, and . . . to persuade her. [He] told her that he was astonished to see that her Highness, who had always shown a resolute spirit in matters of great pith and consequence, should lack it now for an enterprise of so little risk, yet which could prove of so great service to God. . . . Isabella much impressed by his warmth and sincerity, said that she would reconsider. . . . The Queen then sent a messenger for Columbus who overtook him . . . about four miles from where the court was then residing. . . .

"Why the sudden change of mind? One may speculate that . . . the most impressive thing about Columbus's presentation of his case had not been the facts and the arguments, but the man. His dignity, sincerity and absolute certainty must have left their mark on the Queen."[242] Columbus made his way back for another meeting. At the conclusion of this meeting with Isabella, she had agreed to fund Columbus's great enterprise. It then took nearly three months of negotiations to complete the terms of their contract. Columbus's eighteen-year search for the means to complete his enterprise had finally been achieved.

"With the proper credentials and contracts in hand, Columbus proceeded to the port of Palos, at the mouth of the Río Tinto, where his little fleet would be assembled. Because of an obligation owed to the crown, the city of Palos was required to furnish two equipped caravels, the *Pinta* and the *Niña*. Columbus leased a third ship, the *Santa María*.

"Equipping the ships was relatively easy, but manning them was another matter. As experienced as Spanish mariners were, this was not an enterprise that appealed to them. Sea voyages are always uncertain, one sailor observed, but this one was downright foolhardy.[243] Nevertheless, thanks to the support of a veteran sea captain from Palos, Martín Alonso Pinzón, and his brothers, enough crewmen were recruited."[244] Ninety men and boys sailed on the first voyage of discovery.[245]

Columbus, now forty-one years old, was ready to fulfill his mission and sail into the unknown. Columbus left his son Diego at the La Rábida monastery to the care of the Franciscan friars. On August 3, 1492, they left from Spain for the Canary Islands. After the Canary Islands, they knew there would not be another stop until they hit land on the other side of the world. "They had water, wine, provisions, and stores enough to last a year. . . . Columbus was serene and confident of success."[246]

By the middle of September, the crew became very concerned having sailed so far with western winds. They grumbled saying that the eastern winds had been few and would never blow hard enough to return to Spain.[247] At the end of September, the western winds were light, and they sailed slowly west. From September 26 to October 1, they only traveled 382 miles. It had now been two months since leaving Spain and had been over three weeks without any sight of land—a length of time that no man aboard had ever experienced.

Crew members expressed their desire to turn around, believing that continuing west would be certain death. Signs of mutiny began to be manifest as the crew discussed a plan to heave Columbus overboard and pretend that he had fallen in by accident when observing the stars.[248] With each passing day the fear of the crew and their desire to return to Spain grew stronger.

On October 10, sixty-eight days after leaving Spain, the voyage experienced the most critical day of the journey. "They had doubled all previous records for ocean navigation, [and] they had long passed the position where Columbus predicted land would be found."[249] Although they were heading straight for the Bahamas and land was less than two hundred miles ahead, the voyage nearly came to an end.

The captains called for a meeting with Columbus and demanded he change course and return to Spain. They again expressed concern that if they went any further they would never be able to return. Admiral Columbus sought to ease their fear and concern by stating that God had given them the winds to travel thus far, and he would give them the winds to return home.

The officers and crew were not going to take no for an answer and threatened to kill Columbus and turn the ship around themselves if he did not consent. Columbus was determined to continue, so he proposed a compromise saying, "Do me this favor, to stay with me this day and night, and if I don't bring you to land before day . . . cut off my head and you shall return."[250]

Columbus's words of faith and determination softened the crew. The men agreed to persist for three more days. That night, Columbus recorded in the ship log book that he "prayed mightily to the Lord."[251] The abstract of the log book for October 10 reads in part, "The men lost all patience . . . but the Admiral encouraged them in the best manner he could. . . . Having come so far, they had nothing to do but continue on to the Indies, till with the help of our Lord, they should arrive there."

Historian Fernandez de Oviedo wrote of this fateful date, "[Columbus] moved the courage of the weakened minds of those who were about to resort to something shameful . . . and they agreed to do what he commanded and sail three days and not more."[252]

On October 11, the winds were brisk and the ships traveled at their greatest speed of the entire voyage. "Common prudence would have made Columbus heave to [a way of slowing a sail boat's forward progress] for the night, since shoals and rocks invisible by moonlight might lie ahead. . . but the Captain General felt that this was not time for common prudence. He had promised the men to turn back if land were not made within three days, and he intended to make all possible westing in this gale of wind."[253]

Throughout the day on October 11, they spotted land birds and other signs of nearing land, and at 2 a.m. "on October 12th, with the *Pinta* sailing ahead, the weather cleared. In the moonlight one of the sailors on the *Pinta*, Juan Rodriguez Bermejo, saw a white sand beach and land beyond it. After his shout of 'Land! Land!' the *Pinta's* crew raised a flag on its highest mast and fired a cannon."[254] Columbus estimated the land was about six miles away, and preparations were made to proceed to shore.

The abstract of Columbus's journal for October 12 reads in part, "The Admiral went ashore in the . . . ship's boat with the royal standard displayed. . . . And, all having rendered thanks to Our Lord kneeling on the ground, embracing it with tears of joy for the immeasurable mercy of having reached it, the Admiral arose and gave this island the name of San Salvador [Holy Savior]." Columbus wrote of naming the first island, "I named the first of these islands San Salvador, thus bestowing upon it the name of our holy Savior under whose protection I made the discovery."[255]

Christopher Columbus was one of the world's greatest navigators and explorers. His faith, courage, persistence, and unshakable convictions enabled him to fulfill his dream and mission to discover new lands. In the centuries following Columbus's accomplishments, there have been thousands of celebrations held and hundreds of monuments erected in his honor and memory. One of these monuments has inscribed this statement: "To the memory of Christopher Columbus whose high faith and indomitable courage gave to mankind a new world."[256]

Conclusion

Having in our memory models and examples of the attributes of great achievers will assist us in developing and living by these attributes. The first book of this series, *8 Attributes of Great Achievers*, covers attributes one through eight. This volume, *8 Attributes of Great Achievers, Volume II*, covers attributes nine through sixteen. Volume III will cover additional attributes and feature stories from the lives of additional great achievers.

Attribute 1: Responsible
Attribute 2: Creator
Attribute 3: Independent
Attribute 4: Humble
Attribute 5: Honest
Attribute 6: Optimistic
Attribute 7: Vision
Attribute 8: Persistent
Attribute 9: Courage
Attribute 10: Love
Attribute 11: Master of Fundamentals
Attribute 12: Hardworking
Attribute 13: Grateful
Attribute 14: Servant Leader
Attribute 15: Innovator
Attribute 16: Mission Driven

I hope that this book has been enjoyable and helpful to you. I would love to hear from you. Please tell me what you enjoyed about the book and how it has impacted your life.

Cameron C. Taylor
CCT@CameronCTaylor.com

About the Author

Cameron C. Taylor is a best-selling author, highly sought-after speaker, and entrepreneur. Cameron is the author of the books *Preserve, Protect, and Defend*; *Does Your Bag Have Holes? 24 Truths That Lead to Financial and Spiritual Freedom*; *8 Attributes of Great Achievers*; and *Twelve Paradoxes of the Gospel*. Cameron graduated with honors from business school and is the founder of several successful companies and charities. He is a founder of The Glorious Cause of America Institute and serves on its board of directors. Cameron is a recipient of the Circle of Honor Award for being an "exceptional example of honor, integrity, and commitment." He lives in Idaho with his wife and children. Cameron is a gifted teacher who has been invited to speak at hundreds of meetings with excellent reviews.

Cameron's books and lectures have been endorsed by Ken Blanchard, co-author of *The One Minute Manager*; Dr. Stephen R. Covey, author of *The Seven Habits of Highly Effective People*; Billionaire Jon Huntsman, Sr.; Rich DeVos, owner of the Orlando Magic; William Danko, PhD, co-author of *The Millionaire Next Door*; and many others.

Acknowledgements

I would like to thank the many people who helped with the completion of this book. I would like to express individual thanks:

To Paula Taylor. I am greatly blessed to be married to Paula. She is a woman of many, many talents. She has played a key role in the writing and editing of each of my books. I appreciate her constant and enduring support.

To Todd Thompson for the cover art and book design—he is a brilliant designer who is fantastic to work with.

To Jim Jones. He is a gifted writer. I appreciate his efforts editing the book. Jim is a man of service.

To Keri Norman. I have worked with Keri for many years now, and she is a loyal, dedicated friend who gets things done.

To Hillary Mousley and Catherine Christensen for their work as editors.

Endnotes

1. Jim Collin, *Good to Great* (New York: Harper Collins, 2001), 51.
2. Henry David Thoreau, *Thoreau's Thoughts* (Boston: Houghton, Mifflin and Company, 1890), 11.
3. Jack Mayer, *Life in a Jar* (Middlebury, VT: Long Trail Press, 2011), 124.
4. Jack Mayer, *Life in a Jar* (Middlebury, VT: Long Trail Press, 2011), 211.
5. Jack Mayer, *Life in a Jar* (Middlebury, VT: Long Trail Press, 2011), 297.
6. Jack Mayer, *Life in a Jar* (Middlebury, VT: Long Trail Press, 2011), 229.
7. Jack Mayer, *Life in a Jar* (Middlebury, VT: Long Trail Press, 2011), 226.
8. Jack Mayer, *Life in a Jar* (Middlebury, VT: Long Trail Press, 2011), 231-232.
9. Jack Mayer, *Life in a Jar* (Middlebury, VT: Long Trail Press, 2011), 232-233.
10. Jack Mayer, *Life in a Jar* (Middlebury, VT: Long Trail Press, 2011), 297.
11. Jack Mayer, *Life in a Jar* (Middlebury, VT: Long Trail Press, 2011), 298-299.
12. Jack Mayer, *Life in a Jar* (Middlebury, VT: Long Trail Press, 2011), 323.
13. Jack Mayer, *Life in a Jar* (Middlebury, VT: Long Trail Press, 2011), 219, 141.
14. Jack Mayer, *Life in a Jar* (Middlebury, VT: Long Trail Press, 2011), 322.
15. John McCain, *Why Courage Matters* (New York: Random House, 2004), 206.
16. Jack Mayer, *Life in a Jar* (Middlebury, VT: Long Trail Press, 2011), 105.
17. Jack Mayer, *Life in a Jar* (Middlebury, VT: Long Trail Press, 2011), 105.
18. Stephen R. Covey, *The Seven Habits of Highly Effective People* (New York: Simon & Schuster, 1989), 199.
19. Jack Welch, *Jack, Straight from the Gut* (New York, NY: Warner Business Books, 2001), 125.
20. Richard Carlson, *Don't Sweat the Small Stuff for Men* (New York, NY: Hyperion, 2001), 233.
21. Robert Hessen, *Steel Titan: The Life of Charles M. Schwab* (Pittsburg, PA: University of Pittsburgh Press, 1975), 3.
22. Robert Hessen, *Steel Titan: The Life of Charles M. Schwab* (Pittsburg, PA: University of Pittsburgh Press, 1975), 3.
23. Robert Hessen, *Steel Titan: The Life of Charles M. Schwab* (Pittsburg, PA: University of Pittsburgh Press, 1975), 132.
24. Robert Hessen, *Steel Titan: The Life of Charles M. Schwab* (Pittsburg, PA: University of Pittsburgh Press, 1975), 253.
25. Robert Hessen, *Steel Titan: The Life of Charles M. Schwab* (Pittsburg, PA: University of Pittsburgh Press, 1975), 124.
26. Kathleen Parker, "A Sprig of Verbena and the Gifts of a Great Teacher," *Washington Post*, April 14, 2010.
27. Don Soderquist, *Live, Learn, Lead to Make a Difference* (Nashville, TN: Countryman, 2006), 112-115.

28. Tony Dungy and Nathan Whitaker, *Quiet Strength* (Carol Stream, IL: Tyndale House Publishers, 2008), 137-138.
29. Proverbs 18:13, King James Version.
30. Gary Chapman, *The 5 Love Languages* (Chicago, IL: Northfield Publishing, 2010), 75-77.
31. Gary Chapman, Paul White, *The 5 Love Languages of Appreciation in the Workplace* (Chicago, IL: Northfield Publishing, 2011), 93.
32. Gary Chapman, Paul White, *The 5 Love Languages of Appreciation in the Workplace* (Chicago, IL: Northfield Publishing, 2011), 93.
33. H. Burke Peterson, "Removing the Poison of an Unforgiving Spirit," *Ensign*, Nov. 1983, p. 59
34. Jon M. Huntsman, *Winners Never Cheat* (Upper Saddle River, NJ: Wharton School Publishing, 2005), 109, 113.
35. Warren G. Bennis, Burt Nanus, *Leaders: Strategies for Taking Charge* (New York: HarperCollins, 2003), 70.
36. Michael Pearn, Chris Mulrooney, and Tim Payne, *Ending the Blame Culture* (Brookfield, VT, Gower Publishing, 1998), 11-12.
37. Adrian Gostick and Chester Elton, *The Carrot Principle* (New York, NY: Free Press, 2009), 7.
38. Cindy Ventrice, *Make Their Day!* (San Francisco, CA: Berrett-Koehler Publishers, 2009), 4.
39. Tony Dungy and Nathan Whitaker, *Quiet Strength* (Carol Stream, IL: Tyndale House Publishers, 2008), 105.
40. Dr. Steve Franklin quoted in Pat Williams with David Winbish, *How to Be Like Coach Wooden* (Deerfield Beach, FL: Health Communications, 2006), 210.
41. Booker T. Washington quoted in Jim Canterucci, *Personal Brilliance* (New York: AMACOM, 2005), 149.
42. John Wooden with Jack Tobin, *They Call Me Coach* (New York: McGraw-Hill Companies, 2004), 76-78.
43. John Wooden with Steve Jamison, *Wooden: A Lifetime of Observations and Reflections On and Off the Court* (New York: McGraw-Hill, 1997), 191.
44. John Wooden with Steve Jamison, *My Personal Best* (New York: McGraw-Hill, 2004), 140.
45. John Wooden with Steve Jamison, *My Personal Best* (New York: McGraw-Hill, 2004), 145, 106.
46. John Wooden with Steve Jamison, *Wooden: A Lifetime of Observations and Reflections On and Off the Court* (New York: McGraw-Hill, 1997),; Swen Nater and Ronald Gallimore, *You Haven't Taught until They Have Learned: John Wooden's Teaching Principles and Practices* (Morgantown, WV: Fitness Information Technology, 2005), 91; John Wooden and Steve Jamison, *Wooden on Leadership* (New York: McGraw-Hill, 2005), 135.

47. John Wooden and Steve Jamison, *Wooden on Leadership* (New York: McGraw-Hill, 2005), 136.
48. Pat Williams with David Winbish, *How to Be Like Coach Wooden* (Deerfield Beach, FL: Health Communications, 2006), 72.
49. Pat Williams with David Winbish, *How to Be Like Coach Wooden* (Deerfield Beach, FL: Health Communications, 2006), 80.
50. Pat Williams with David Winbish, *How to Be Like Coach Wooden* (Deerfield Beach, FL: Health Communications, 2006), 154.
51. Pat Williams with David Winbish, *How to Be Like Coach Wooden* (Deerfield Beach, FL: Health Communications, 2006), 195.
52. Pat Williams with David Winbish, *How to Be Like Coach Wooden* (Deerfield Beach, FL: Health Communications, 2006), 72.
53. Pat Williams with David Winbish, *How to Be Like Coach Wooden* (Deerfield Beach, FL: Health Communications, 2006), 151.
54. Pat Williams with David Winbish, *How to Be Like Coach Wooden* (Deerfield Beach, FL: Health Communications, 2006), 73.
55. Pat Williams with David Winbish, *How to Be Like Coach Wooden* (Deerfield Beach, FL: Health Communications, 2006), 153–54.
56. Neville L. Johnson, *The John Wooden Pyramid of Success* (Los Angeles: Cool Titles, 2003), 331, 191.
57. Pat Williams with David Winbish, *How to Be Like Coach Wooden* (Deerfield Beach, FL: Health Communications, 2006), 205.
58. Vice Admiral James B. Stockdale, *A Vietnam Experience* (Stanford, CA, Hoover Press, 1984), 28.
59. Jim Collin, *Good to Great* (New York: Harper Collins, 2001), 84-85.
60. Viktor E. Frankl, *Man's Search for Meaning* (New York: Pocket Books, 1984), 96.
61. Norman Wood, *Lives of Famous Indian Chiefs* (Aurora, IL: American Indian Historical Publishing Company, 1906), 704-706.
62. Rhonda Byrne, *The Secret* (New York: Atria Books, 2006), 95.
63. Rhonda Byrne, *The Secret* (New York: Atria Books, 2006), 7.
64. Rhonda Byrne, *The Secret* (New York: Atria Books, 2006), 59.
65. Rhonda Byrne, *The Secret* (New York: Atria Books, 2006), 102.
66. Rhonda Byrne, *The Secret* (New York: Atria Books, 2006), 131.
67. Rhonda Byrne, *The Secret* (New York: Atria Books, 2006), 68, 63.
68. Rhonda Byrne, *The Secret* (New York: Atria Books, 2006), 41.
69. Rhonda Byrne, *The Secret* (New York: Atria Books, 2006), 68.
70. Rhonda Byrne, *The Secret* (New York: Atria Books, 2006), 48, 47.
71. Rhonda Byrne, *The Secret* (New York: Atria Books, 2006), 51, 55.
72. Rhonda Byrne, *The Secret* (New York: Atria Books, 2006), ix, 82.
73. Harold C. Livesay, *American Made* (New York: Pearson-Longman, 2007), 122.

74. *Academic American Encyclopedia* (Princeton, NJ: Arete Publishing Co., 1980), 212.
75. "Wright Brothers", Wikipedia. Retrieved December 7, 2006, from http://en.wikipedia.org/wiki/Wright_brothers
76. Rhonda Byrne, *The Secret* (New York: Atria Books, 2006), 119.
77. Rhonda Byrne, *The Secret* (New York: Atria Books, 2006), 85, 108, 118, 178, 179, 184.
78. Simon Firth, "Nearly 40 Years Later, A Bing Study Is Still Going," *The Bing Times*, November 2005, p. 7
79. Rhonda Byrne, *The Secret* (New York: Atria Books, 2006), 144, 169, 184.
80. William S. Sahakian, Mabel Lewis Sahakian, *Ideas of the Great Philosophers* (New York: Barnes & Noble Books, 1993), 28.
81. F. Nephi Grigg, *Breefs by Neef* (Salt Lake City, UT: F. Nephi Grigg, 1985).
82. Jeff Benedict, *How to Build a Business Warren Buffet Would Buy* (Salt Lake City, UT: Shadow Mountain, 2009), 2, 32.
83. Jeff Benedict, *How to Build a Business Warren Buffet Would Buy* (Salt Lake City, UT: Shadow Mountain, 2009), 43.
84. Jeff Benedict, *How to Build a Business Warren Buffet Would Buy* (Salt Lake City, UT: Shadow Mountain, 2009), 146.
85. Jeff Benedict, *How to Build a Business Warren Buffet Would Buy* (Salt Lake City, UT: Shadow Mountain, 2009), 146.
86. Michael Silver, "Straight Shooter," *Sports Illustrated*, April 07, 1997.
87. Tony Dungy and Nathan Whitaker, *Quiet Strength* (Carol Stream, IL: Tyndale House Publishers, 2008), 29.
88. Michael Silver, "Straight Shooter," *Sports Illustrated*, April 07, 1997.
89. Bill Gates, *The Road Ahead* (New York: Viking, 1995), 12.
90. Bill Gates, *The Road Ahead* (New York: Viking, 1995), 4.
91. Bill Gates, *The Road Ahead* (New York: Viking, 1995), 15.
92. Bill Gates, *The Road Ahead* (New York: Viking, 1995), 14.
93. Bill Gates, *The Road Ahead* (New York: Viking, 1995), 14.
94. Bill Gates, *The Road Ahead* (New York: Viking, 1995), 15.
95. Bill Gates, *The Road Ahead* (New York: Viking, 1995), 16.
96. Paul Allen, *Idea Man* (New York: Penguin Group, 1991), 8-9.
97. Bill Gates, *The Road Ahead* (New York: Viking, 1995), 17.
98. Daniel Gross, *Forbes Greatest Business Stories of All Times* (New York: John Wiley & Sons, 1996), 339.
99. Bill Gates, *The Road Ahead* (New York: Viking, 1995), 18.
100. Daniel Gross, *Forbes Greatest Business Stories of All Times* (New York: John Wiley & Sons, 1996), 345.
101. Daniel Gross, *Forbes Greatest Business Stories of All Times* (New York: John Wiley & Sons, 1996), 340; Paul Allen, *Idea Man* (New York: Penguin Group, 1991), 116.

102. Paul Allen, *Idea Man* (New York: Penguin Group, 1991), 2.

103. Paul Allen, *Idea Man* (New York: Penguin Group, 1991), 3.

104. Roger Bannister, *The Four-Minute Mile* (Guilford, CT: The Globe Pequot Press, 1981), 35.

105. Roger Bannister, *The Four-Minute Mile* (Guilford, CT: The Globe Pequot Press, 1981), 35.

106. Roger Bannister, *The Four-Minute Mile* (Guilford, CT: The Globe Pequot Press, 1981), 45, 48.

107. Roger Bannister, *The Four-Minute Mile* (Guilford, CT: The Globe Pequot Press, 1981), 50.

108. Roger Bannister, *The Four-Minute Mile* (Guilford, CT: The Globe Pequot Press, 1981), 50.

109. Roger Bannister, *The Four-Minute Mile* (Guilford, CT: The Globe Pequot Press, 1981), 58-59.

110. Roger Bannister, *The Four-Minute Mile* (Guilford, CT: The Globe Pequot Press, 1981), 97-98.

111. Roger Bannister, *The Four-Minute Mile* (Guilford, CT: The Globe Pequot Press, 1981), 156, 159.

112. Roger Bannister, *The Four-Minute Mile* (Guilford, CT: The Globe Pequot Press, 1981), 161-162.

113. Roger Bannister, *The Four-Minute Mile* (Guilford, CT: The Globe Pequot Press, 1981), 175.

114. Roger Bannister, *The Four-Minute Mile* (Guilford, CT: The Globe Pequot Press, 1981), 176-178.

115. Roger Bannister, *The Four-Minute Mile* (Guilford, CT: The Globe Pequot Press, 1981), 183.

116. Roger Bannister, *The Four-Minute Mile* (Guilford, CT: The Globe Pequot Press, 1981), 187-188.

117. Roger Bannister, *The Four-Minute Mile* (Guilford, CT: The Globe Pequot Press, 1981), 201.

118. Roger Bannister, *The Four-Minute Mile* (Guilford, CT: The Globe Pequot Press, 1981), 204.

119. Roger Bannister, *The Four-Minute Mile* (Guilford, CT: The Globe Pequot Press, 1981), 209.

120. Roger Bannister, *The Four-Minute Mile* (Guilford, CT: The Globe Pequot Press, 1981), 213-215.

121. Bruce Lowitt, "Bannister Stuns World with 4-Minute Mile" *St. Petersburg Times*, December 17, 1999.

122. David M. Ewalt and Lacey Rose, "The Greatest Individual Athletic Achievements," *Forbes*, January 29, 2008.

123. Shad Helmstetter, *What to Say When You Talk to Your Self* (New York: Pocket Books, 1986), 20.

124. Roger Bannister, *The Four-Minute Mile* (Guilford, CT: The Globe Pequot Press, 1981), 231, 238.

125. Roger Bannister, *The Four-Minute Mile* (Guilford, CT: The Globe Pequot Press, 1981), viii.

126. Don Soderquist, *Live Learn Lead to Make a Difference* (Nashville, TN: J. Countryman, 2006), 19.

127. David A. Adler, Lou Gehrig, *The Luckiest Man* (Orlando, FL: Gulliver Books, 1997).

128. Corrie ten Boom, with John and Elizabeth Sherrill, *The Hiding Place* (New York: Doubleday Direct, 1995), 186-187, 197.

129. Noelle C. Nelson and Jeannine Lemare Calaba, *The Power of Appreciation* (Hillsboro, OR: Beyond Words Publishing, 2003), xi.

130. Jim Collins, *Good to Great* (New York: HarperCollins, 2001), 12, 21.

131. Blaine Lee, *The Power Principle* (New York: Simon & Schuster, 1997), 132.

132. Walter Payton, *Never Die Easy* (New York: Villard Books, 2000), 248.

133. Michael Jordan, *I Can't Accept Not Trying* (Chicago, IL: Rare Air, 1994) 14.

134. John Wooden with Steve Jamison, *My Personal Best* (New York: McGraw-Hill, 2004), 114-115.

135. John Wooden with Steve Jamison, *My Personal Best* (New York: McGraw-Hill, 2004), 119.

136. John Wooden with Steve Jamison, *My Personal Best* (New York: McGraw-Hill, 2004), 120-123, 195.

137. John Wooden with Steve Jamison, *My Personal Best* (New York: McGraw-Hill, 2004), 4.

138. C.S. Lewis, *Mere Christianity* (New York: Simon & Schuster, 1996), 110.

139. Sam Walton, *Sam Walton* (New York: Doubleday, 1992), 234.

140. C.S. Lewis, *Mere Christianity* (New York: Simon & Schuster, 1996), 111.

141. C.S. Lewis, *Mere Christianity* (New York: Simon & Schuster, 1996), 110.

142. Alan L. Chisholm, "Coping With Envy," *Psychotherapy & Spirituality Institute*, retrieved January 11, 2007, from http://www.mindspirit.org/psiqa04.htm.

143. Genesis 37:3–4, King James Version.

144. Acts 7:9, King James Version.

145. C.S. Lewis, *Mere Christianity* (New York: Simon & Schuster, 1996), 114.

146. Edward Charles M'Guire, *The Religious Opinions and Character of Washington* (New York: Harper & Brothers, 1836), 330-31.

147. B. J. Losing, *Signers of the Declaration of Independence* (New York: George F. Colledge & Brother, 1848), 167.

148. Benjamin Franklin, *Memoirs of Benjamin Franklin, Volume I* (Philadelphia: McCarty & Davis, 1834), 57.

149. Jared Sparks, *The Writing of George Washington, Volume II* (Boston: Russel, Osiorne, and Metcalf, 1834), 468.

150. The sash Washington received from General Braddock is in Mount Vernon's

collection but is not currently on view. In recent years, the sash has been in several traveling exhibitions, including "George Washington: The Man Behind the Myths" and "Treasures from Mount Vernon." Because the sash was on view for a long period of time and is in delicate condition, Mount Vernon has restricted it from display for a number of years. Textiles are particularly vulnerable to light damage and can only be on exhibit for brief periods (a general rule that many museums follow is an item made of silk—like Braddock's sash—should only be on view 3 months for every 10 years). In order to protect the sash for future generations, it is currently being stored in low light conditions.

151. Jay A. Parry and Andrew M. Allison, *The Real George Washington* (National Center for Constitutional Studies, 1991), xviii.

152. Jay A. Parry and Andrew M. Allison, *The Real George Washington* (National Center for Constitutional Studies, 1991), 78.

153. William Hickey, *The Constitution of the United States of America* (Philadelphia, 1851), 201-202.

154. George Washington and Jared Sparks, *The Writings of George Washington, Volume II* (New York: Harper & Brothers, 1847), 405.

155. John Marshall, *The Life of George Washington* (New York: Derby & Jackson, 1857), 27.

156. *The Executive Documents of the Senate of the United States* (Washington, DC: U.S. Government Printing Office, 1888) Enclosure 42, Washington Papers, 66.

157. Gerald M. Carbone, Nathanael Greene: *A Biography of the American Revolution* (New York: Palgrave Macmillan, 2010), 24.

158. Jay A. Parry and Andrew M. Allison, *The Real George Washington* (National Center for Constitutional Studies, 1991), 414-415.

159. George Washington, *The life of General Washington: First President of the United States, Volume 1* (London: Office of the National Illustrated Library, 1852), 101.

160. Appleton P.C. Griffin and William Coolidge Lane, *A Catalogue of the Washington Collection in the Boston Athenæum* (Boston: The Boston Athenæum, 1897), vii.

161. Jared Sparks, *The Writings of George Washington , Volume III* (Boston: Russel, Odiorne, and Metcalf and Hillard, Gray, and Co., 1834), 152-153.

162. *The Pennsylvania Magazine of History and Biography, Volume 20* (Philadelphia, PA, Historical Society of Pennsylvania, 1896), 515-516.

163. From speech "The Glorious Cause of America" delivered by David McCullough on September 27, 2005 at Brigham Young University in Provo, UT.

164. John Marshall, *The Life of George Washington, Volume II* (London: Richard Phillips, 1804), 424.

165. From speech "The Glorious Cause of America" delivered by David

McCullough on September 27, 2005 at Brigham Young University in Provo, UT.

166. Worthington Chauncey Ford, *George Washington, Volume 2* (New York: Goupil & Co. and Charles Scribner's Sons, 1900), 107.

167. Elizabeth Bryant Johnson, *George Washington Day by Day* (New York: The Baker & Taylor Co., 1895), 30.

168. David Ridgely, *Annals of Annapolis* (Baltimore: Cushing & Brother, 1841), 211. Text of a letter by George Washington following the Revolutionary War: "Permit me, gentlemen, to offer you my sincere thanks for your congratulations on the happy events of peace, and the establishment of our independence. If my conduct throughout the war has merited the confidence of my fellow citizens, and has been instrumental in obtaining for my country the blessings of peace and freedom, I owe it to that Supreme Being, who guides the hearts of all: who has so signally interposed his aid in every stage of the contest, and who has graciously been pleased to bestow on me the greatest of earthly rewards—the approbation and affections of a free people. Though I retire from the employments of public life, I shall never cease to entertain the most anxious care for the welfare of my country. May the Almighty dispose the heart of every citizen of the United States to improve the great prospect of happiness before us! And may you, gentlemen, and the inhabitants of this city, long enjoy every felicity this world can afford."

169. Glen Beck, *Being George Washington* (New York: Simon and Schuster, 2011), 286.

170. John Marshall, *The Life of George Washington, Volume II* (London: Richard Phillips, 1804), 424.

171. Thomas Jefferson and Henry Augustine Washington (editor), *The Writings of Thomas Jefferson, Volume I* (Washington, DC: Taylor& Maury, 1853), 328.

172. Charles W. Upham, *The Life of Washington, in the Form of an Autobiography, Volume II* (Boston: Marsh, Capen, Lyon, and Webb, 1840), 121.

173. Benson J. Lossing, *Seventeen Hundred and Seventy-six, or The War of Independence* (New York: Edward Walker, 1848), 471.

174. John Marshall, *The Life of George Washington, Volume II* (Philadelphia: James Crissy, 1843), 125.

175. Francis S. Drake, *Life and Correspondence of Henry Knox* (Boston: Samuel G. Drake, 1873), 144.

176. Jay A. Parry and Andrew M. Allison, *The Real George Washington* (National Center for Constitutional Studies, 1991), 497-498.

177. Thomas Prichard Rossiter, Louis Remy Mignot, *A Description of the Picture of the Home of Washington After the War* (New York: D. Appleton and Company, 1859), 33.

178. *Documentary History of the Constitution of the United States of America, Volume IV* (Washington, DC: Department of the State, 1905), 359. Letter from

Gouverneur Morris to Washington reads in part, "I will add my Conviction that of all Men you are best fitted to fill that Office. Your cool steady Temper is indispensably necessary to give a firm and manly Tone to the new Government."

179. John Marshall, *The Life of George Washington, Volume II* (Philadelphia: James Crissy, 1843), 136.

180. *American State Papers: Documents, Legislative and Executive, of the Congress of the United States* (Washington, DC: Gales and Seaton, 1834), 6.

181. *American State Papers: Documents, Legislative and Executive, of the Congress of the United States, Volume I* (Washington, DC: Gales and Seaton, 1833), 10.

182. Jay A. Parry and Andrew M. Allison, *The Real George Washington* (National Center for Constitutional Studies, 1991), 605.

183. F.L. Patton (Editor), *The Princeton University Bulletin, Volumes IX to XII* (Princeton, NJ: The Princeton University Press), 55.

184. Stanislaus Vincent Henkels, *An Extraordinary Collection of Washington's Letters, Washington Relics, Revolutionary Documents and the Rarest Works on American History* (Times Printing House, 1891), 5.

185. Horatio Hastings Weld, *Pictorial Life of George Washington* (Philadelphia: Lindsay and Blakiston, 1846), 182.

186. Michael and Jana Novak, *Washington's God* (New York: Basic Books, 2006), 4-5.

187. Edwin A. Locke, *The Essence of Leadership* (New York: Lexington Books, 1991), 79.

188. Elma G. Farnsworth, *Distant Vision* (Salt Lake City, UT: PemberlyKent Publishers, 1990), 27.

189. Elma G. Farnsworth, *Distant Vision* (Salt Lake City, UT: PemberlyKent Publishers, 1990), 33.

190. Evan I. Schwartz, *The Last Lone Inventor* (New York: HarperCollins, 2002), 14-15.

191. Evan I. Schwartz, *The Last Lone Inventor* (New York: HarperCollins, 2002), 16.

192. Evan I. Schwartz, *The Last Lone Inventor* (New York: HarperCollins, 2002), 21.

193. Elma G. Farnsworth, *Distant Vision* (Salt Lake City, UT: PemberlyKent Publishers, 1990), 39.

194. Elma G. Farnsworth, *Distant Vision* (Salt Lake City, UT: PemberlyKent Publishers, 1990), 46.

195. George Everson, *The Story of Television: The Life of Philo T. Farnsworth* (New York: W.W. Norton & Company, 1949), 40.

196. George Everson, *The Story of Television: The Life of Philo T. Farnsworth* (New York: W.W. Norton & Company, 1949), 41.

197. George Everson, *The Story of Television: The Life of Philo T. Farnsworth* (New York: W.W. Norton & Company, 1949), 41.

198. George Everson, *The Story of Television: The Life of Philo T. Farnsworth* (New

York: W.W. Norton & Company, 1949), 45.

199. George Everson, *The Story of Television: The Life of Philo T. Farnsworth* (New York: W.W. Norton & Company, 1949), 46.

200. Elma G. Farnsworth, *Distant Vision* (Salt Lake City, UT: PemberlyKent Publishers, 1990), 9.

201. Elma G. Farnsworth, *Distant Vision* (Salt Lake City, UT: PemberlyKent Publishers, 1990), 9.

202. Elma G. Farnsworth, *Distant Vision* (Salt Lake City, UT: PemberlyKent Publishers, 1990), 22.

203. George Everson, *The Story of Television: The Life of Philo T. Farnsworth* (New York: W.W. Norton & Company, 1949), 51-52.

204. Evan I. Schwartz, *The Last Lone Inventor* (New York: HarperCollins, 2002), 84.

205. George Everson, *The Story of Television: The Life of Philo T. Farnsworth* (New York: W.W. Norton & Company, 1949), 62.

206. George Everson, *The Story of Television: The Life of Philo T. Farnsworth* (New York: W.W. Norton & Company, 1949), 64.

207. George Everson, *The Story of Television: The Life of Philo T. Farnsworth*(New York: W.W. Norton & Company, 1949), 64-72.

208. George Everson, *The Story of Television: The Life of Philo T. Farnsworth* (New York: W.W. Norton & Company, 1949), 80.

209. Paul Schatzkin, *The Boy Who Invented Television* (Silver Spring, MD: Teamcom Books, 2002), 249.

210. Elma G. Farnsworth, *Distant Vision* (Salt Lake City, UT: PemberlyKent Publishers, 1990), xii.

211. Evan I. Schwartz, *The Last Lone Inventor* (New York: HarperCollins, 2002), 126.

212. Evan I. Schwartz, *The Last Lone Inventor* (New York: HarperCollins, 2002), 127.

213. George Everson, *The Story of Television: The Life of Philo T. Farnsworth* (New York: W.W. Norton & Company, 1949), 91.

214. Elma G. Farnsworth, *Distant Vision* (Salt Lake City, UT: PemberlyKent Publishers, 1990), 131-132.

215. Evan I. Schwartz, *The Last Lone Inventor* (New York: HarperCollins, 2002), 140.

216. Elma G. Farnsworth, *Distant Vision* (Salt Lake City, UT: PemberlyKent Publishers, 1990), 267.

217. Elma G. Farnsworth, *Distant Vision* (Salt Lake City, UT: PemberlyKent Publishers, 1990), 215.

218. *Biographical Note/Historical Note*. University of Utah, J. Willard Marriot Library Marriott Library, Special Collections. Retrieved March 15, 2013 from http://content.lib.utah.edu/cdm/ref/collection/UU_EAD/id/2160#section_bioghist

219. Elma G. Farnsworth, *Distant Vision* (Salt Lake City, UT: PemberlyKent Publishers, 1990), 333.

220. Elma G. Farnsworth, *Distant Vision* (Salt Lake City, UT: PemberlyKent Publishers, 1990), 215.

221. *Biographical Note/Historical Note.* University of Utah, J. Willard Marriot Library Marriott Library, Special Collections. Retrieved March 15, 2013 from http://content.lib.utah.edu/cdm/ref/collection/UU_EAD/id/2160#section_bioghist

222. Victor Frankl, *Man's Search for Meaning* (Boston, MA: Beacon Press, 1959), 113.

223. Herb Miller, *Money Is Everything* (Nashville, TN: Discipleship Resources, 1994), 19.

224. Stephen R. Covey, *The Seven Habits of Highly Effective People* (New York: Simon & Schuster, 2004), 128-29.

225. Laurie Beth Jones, *The Path* (New York, NY: Hyperion, 1996), 26.

226. Paul Allen, *Idea Man* (New York: Penguin Group, 1991), 31-32.

227. Don Soderquist, *Live Learn Lead to Make a Difference* (Nashville, TN: J. Countryman, 2006), 121.

228. Samuel Eliot Morison, *Admiral of the Ocean Sea* (New York: MJF Books, 1942), 49-50.

229. Samuel Eliot Morison, *Admiral of the Ocean Sea* (New York: MJF Books, 1942), 69.

230. Samuel Eliot Morison, *Admiral of the Ocean Sea* (New York: MJF Books, 1942), 73.

231. Ferdinand Columbus, *The Life of the Admiral Christopher Columbus by His Son Ferdinand* (New Brunswick: Rutgers University Press, 1959), 59.

232. De Lamar Jensen, "Columbus and the Hand of God," *Ensign*, Oct. 1992.

233. Samuel Eliot Morison, *Admiral of the Ocean Sea* (New York: MJF Books, 1942), 75.

234. Samuel Eliot Morison, *Admiral of the Ocean Sea* (New York: MJF Books, 1942), 76.

235. De Lamar Jensen, "Columbus and the Hand of God," *Ensign*, Oct. 1992.

236. Samuel Eliot Morison, *Admiral of the Ocean Sea* (New York: MJF Books, 1942), 47.

237. Kay Brigham, *Christopher Columbus: His Life and Discovery in the Light of His Prophecies* (Terrassa, Barcelona, Spain: CLIE Publishers, 1990), 170.

238. Samuel Eliot Morison, *Admiral of the Ocean Sea* (New York: MJF Books, 1942), 91.

239. Samuel Eliot Morison, *Admiral of the Ocean Sea* (New York: MJF Books, 1942), 97.

240. Jacob Wassermann, *Columbus, Don Quixote of the Seas* (Boston: Little, Brown and Co., 1930), 19–20.

241. Samuel Eliot Morison, *Admiral of the Ocean Sea* (New York: MJF Books, 1942), 97-99.

242. Samuel Eliot Morison, *Admiral of the Ocean Sea* (New York: MJF Books, 1942), 102-103.

243. Pleitos colombinos, quoted in Paolo Emilio Taviani, *Christopher Columbus: the Grand Design* (London: Orbis, 1985), 143–44, 204.

244. De Lamar Jensen, "Columbus and the Hand of God," *Ensign*, Oct. 1992.

245. Samuel Eliot Morison, *Admiral of the Ocean Sea* (New York: MJF Books, 1942), 141.

246. Samuel Eliot Morison, *Admiral of the Ocean Sea* (New York: MJF Books, 1942), 197.

247. The ship log of September 22 reads, "From time to time we faced a contrary wind. This relieved some of the crew, for until now the wind has been behind us all the time which caused them to worry about how we should ever get back to Spain. The ship log of September 23 read, "Even now, some continue to grumble, saying that the wind would never blow hard enough to get them back."

248. Samuel Eliot Morison, *Admiral of the Ocean Sea* (New York: MJF Books, 1942), 208.

249. Samuel Eliot Morison, *Admiral of the Ocean Sea* (New York: MJF Books, 1942), 215.

250. Samuel Eliot Morison, *Admiral of the Ocean Sea* (New York: MJF Books, 1942), 218.

251. Words written by Columbus in his ship log, October 11, 1492; Bill Halamandaris, *The Heart of America: Ten Core Values That Make Our Country Great* (Deerfield Beach, FL: Health Communications, Inc., 2004), 30.

252. Samuel Eliot Morison, *Admiral of the Ocean Sea* (New York: MJF Books, 1942), 220.

253. Samuel Eliot Morison, *Admiral of the Ocean Sea* (New York: MJF Books, 1942), 223.

254. William D. Phillips, Jr. and Carla Rahn Phillips, *The Worlds of Christopher Columbus* (New York: Cambridge University Press, 1992), 152–153.

255. Christopher Columbus, *Personal Narrative of the First Voyage of Columbus to America* (Boston: Thomas B. Wait and Son, 1827), 240. Today San Salvador Island is an island in the Bahamas and has a population of approximately about 1,000 and is home to the Club Med Columbus Isle resort.

256. Inscription found on the Columbus Fountain located at Union Station in Washington, D.C.

8 Attributes of Great Achievers

By Cameron C. Taylor

This book is filled with inspiring stories from the lives of great achievers past and present including Gandhi, the Wright Brothers, Abraham Lincoln, Winston Churchill, Walt Disney, Sam Walton, Jon Huntsman, Warren Buffet, Christopher Columbus, George Washington, Benjamin Franklin, and others. From this book, you will learn:

- How Winston Churchill's optimism enabled England to withstand the attacks of Hitler and eventually win the war.
- How Walt Disney used the power of goals to create (Snow White, Disneyland, etc.) and make his dreams come true.
- Why George Washington carried a bloody sash with him throughout his life.
- Powerful experiences from the Wright Brothers on taking the initiative.
- Stories on honesty from billionaire Jon Huntsman that illustrate nice guys really can, and do, finish first in life.
- Fifteen principles to build strong, uplifting relationships.
- How a World War II concentration camp prisoner was able to remain strong, happy, and peaceful even in the worst of environments.
- How Gandhi's "experiment with truth" enabled him to go from a shy boy and an average man, to the leader of 500 million people who called him "The Great Soul."

- How top CEOs use the principle of abundance to increase productivity and profits.
- Inspiring stories on persistence and overcoming failures from the Wright Brothers, Columbus, Sam Walton, Sylvester Stallone, Colonel Sanders, and the lives of other great achievers.

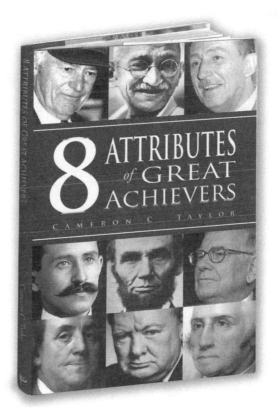

Available at: www.CameronCTaylor.com

Does Your Bag Have Holes?
24 Truths That Lead to Financial and Spiritual Freedom
By Cameron C. Taylor

Book Review by Joi Sigers

Does Your Bag Have Holes? is what can only be called a perfect book. The lessons, ideals, illustrations, and quotes in this book have the power to change every single aspect of the reader's life for the better. What Cameron gives his readers in *Does Your Bag Have Holes?* is unique. The book contains information that you will not find anywhere else. It's a book that you'll find yourself returning to again and again and again. It's a book you won't just read, you'll experience it.

The world would be a much better place if Cameron C. Taylor wrote more books! Not only is he a fantastic author, he's a great teacher and motivator. I love to see someone doing what they were meant to do. There's a certain beauty about it. Whether it's Faith Hill singing, Frank Sinatra dancing, or Serena Williams playing tennis—there's something awe-inspiring when someone has found what they were meant to do, and they carry it out as beautifully as nature knew they would. Cameron was meant to write, and he does so beautifully. He writes with humor, insight, and profound wisdom.

I took countless notes while reading the book and his teachings have had a great impact upon my life. I came across so many different stories (with illustrations) that I wanted to scan/type in and send to the people on my e-mail list. They're that amazing. Then I realized, after I lost count of the number of stories, that it would be much wiser to simply shoot out one widespread e-mail recommending this book and everything in it. I've recommended this book to everyone I know and now would like to recommend it to you!

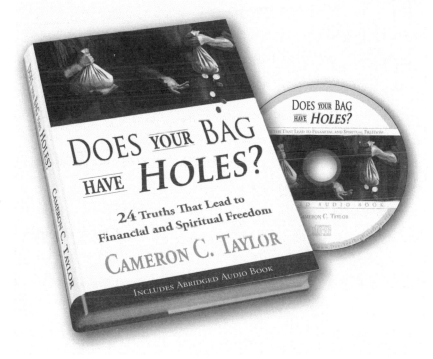

Available at: www.CameronCTaylor.com

Twelve Paradoxes of the Gospel

By Cameron C. Taylor

The gospel of Jesus Christ is filled with paradoxes. Many of God's directions appear to be contrary to logic and reason. On the surface they appear to have the opposite effect of the promised result. This book explores twelve of these gospel paradoxes with powerful scriptures and stories from the lives of faith-filled Christians. In these paradoxical statements are profound truths that lead to happiness in this life and eternal life in the world to come.

- The Paradox of Faith contains insight on faith from the Apostle Peter's experience walking on water with Jesus.
- The Paradox of Performance teaches why the first shall be last; and the last shall be first.
- The Paradox of Leadership shares inspiring stories of servant leadership from the life of Jesus Christ, Abraham Lincoln, and the Founding Fathers.
- The Paradox of Wisdom contains three lessons learned from Balaam's talking donkey found in the book of Numbers.
- The Paradox of Receiving contains insights on prayer and receiving gifts from God.
- The Paradox of Pain answers the question of why bad things happen to good people.
- The Paradox of Forgiveness contains great stories from the life of Leonardo Da Vinci and others on the power of forgiveness.

- The Paradox of Wealth teaches principles every parent must know to raise productive, self-sufficient children and grandchildren.
- The Paradox of Giving shows how giving actually makes you richer.
- The Paradox of Fundamentals teaches how to apply in your life the formula legendary coach John Wooden used to create ten national championship teams in twelve years.

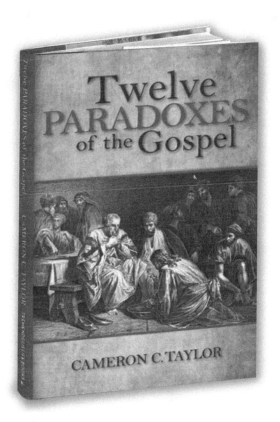

Available at: www.CameronCTaylor.com

Preserve Protect & Defend

By Cameron C. Taylor

While investigating corruption and evil alliances within the American government, an assassination attempt on Vice President Aaron Banner leaves him in a coma. Only a week earlier, Aaron gave his chief of staff, Paula Brackett, an envelope with instructions to, "Open only if something happens to me." Paula soon finds herself fighting not only for her country, but for her life. While Aaron is in a coma, he is transported in time to personally experience key moments in history. Aaron is taught unforgettable lessons from some of the wisest men who have ever lived—George Washington, Christopher Columbus, Benjamin Franklin, Abraham Lincoln, and others. This book beautifully blends remarkable research and details of the founding of America with an inspiring and engaging story.

Comments from Readers

"You beautifully merges history, truth, and an edge of your seat thriller into a book that you cannot put down. *Preserve, Protect and Defend* is one of the best written narratives." -Dale West

"The book *Preserve, Protect and Defend* is amazing! I couldn't stop reading! The suspense and reality of the events that are taking place make you feel like you are right there in the action. Thank you Cameron! I will definitely share this book with everyone I know." -Tom Sathre

"*Preserve, Protect and Defend* was a great read. I'm sixty-one and cried all through it. Thank you for sharing your talents."
-S. Dean Chappell

"Loved your book! So much good information in such a small package. Beautiful." -June Rigby

"I just finished reading your most inspiring book. It has renewed my faith in this country and its people." -Jerry Bakken

"Once I began reading, I could not put it down. This book so closely parallels what is going on in our nation today, it is frightening. I am passing this book around to my family and friends. Keep up the great work!" -Suzanne Tyler

"Mr. Taylor presents a fast-moving story which weaves into the drama the characters and quotes of the Founding Fathers, their vision, and a solution to restoring a Constitutional America. Well done, Mr. Taylor!" -Chris Williams

Available at: www.CameronCTaylor.com